The Six-Gun Mystique
Second Edition

The Six-Gun Mystique
Second Edition

John Cawelti

Bowling Green State University Popular Press
Bowling Green, Ohio 43403

To Katie
who makes all the difference

Contents

Foreword

The original edition of *The Six-Gun Mystique* has been in print for almost fifteen years. It seemed appropriate at this time to bring out a revised edition correcting mistakes in the original printing and adding an analysis of developments in the Western since 1970. This new introduction, together with a bibliography and filmography, are placed at the beginning of this new edition. The original text of *The Six-Gun Mystique* with its appended bibliographies and filmographies follows.

Many of those I acknowledged in the original foreward have continued to discuss the Western with me over the years. I have also discussed aspects of the Western with many people since 1970. There are really too many of these to list, but I would like the following names to stand for the multitudes who have shared their interest and insights into the subject with me: Richard Etulain, Sam Girgus, Delbert Wylder, Ray Merlock, Stuart Kaminsky, Horace Newcomb, Frances M. Nevins, Jr., J. Dudley Andrew, Richard Slotkin, Daniel Aaron, Alan Trachtenberg, Janel Mueller, Thomas Schatz, Howard Lamar, Robert Dykstra, Bernice Slote, William Kittredge, William Bevis, Walter Blair, Gerhard Hoffmann, Gunnar Hallingberg, Virginia Wexman, Alan Slickpoo, J. A. Bryant, Jr., Michael Marsden, Jack Nachbar and Bruce Rosenberg.

I have gained much from several conferences on Western myths, history and literature organized by Oregon State University (Richard Astro) The Sun Valley Center for the Arts and Humanities (James Belson) and the Montana Committee for the Humanities (Richard Chapman). Among the special benefits of these conferences were the chance to meet and talk with persons who had been involved in the making of the Western films including John Ford, Howard Hawks, Clint Eastwood, Iron Eyes Cody, Peter Fonda, Warren Oates, Chief Dan George, Col. Tim McCoy, King Vidor, Delmer Daves, and Duncan Renaldo. Thanks to these people for being so willing to talk about their work.

I've had the privilege of lecturing about the Western at several American and German universities and at the American Studies Research Center in Hyderabad, India. My thanks to the faculty and students at these many institutions for their questions and suggestions.

As always, without the help and encouragement of Ray and Pat Browne, this new edition would not have been possible.

Finally, I have learned the most from constant discussions with my wife, Mary Catherine Flannery Cawelti. This new edition is dedicated to her.

Louisville and Lexington, Kentucky   1984

This long essay deals in a preliminary way with the basic principles of interpretation and explanation relevant to a certain class of cultural materials, the popular formula narrative and drama. Though my attention is focused throughout on the Western, I believe that the general considerations advanced here are equally applicable to the detective story, the spy story, the bestselling romance, the various forms of science-fiction, the gothic thriller and those many other forms of fiction which follow a highly conventionalized pattern. I hope in a later and more extended publication to deal with a number of these other popular forms as well. (cf. *Adventure, Mystery and Romance.*)

My interest in this area grew initially from a personal predilection for detective stories, which led me to wonder just why I and so many other people drew such pleasure and gratification from literary works which many of our most respected critics dismissed as contemptible trash. Though I had long mused upon this question, my theoretical interest in the subject was ignited by an essay on the Western by my colleague and friend Prof. Peter Homans of the Divinity School of the University of Chicago. Since that time I have read essays on the Western, the detective story and other popular forms by the widest variety of people from a large spectrum of disciplinary perspectives: history, literary criticism, various brands of psychology, sociology, journalism, mass communications and political science. The views expressed in these essays were so diverse that I decided it was time to attempt a synthesis by taking some tentative steps toward an interdisciplinary method of interpreting these forms of popular culture. For this reason my essay deals not only with the form of the Western but with the theoretical problem of differing principles of analysis and explanation of this form.

Portions of this essay have appeared in earlier versions in *Studies in Public Communication, The Journal of Popular Culture* and *Western American Literature.* I'm grateful to the editors of those journals for originally giving my views a hearing and for permitting me to weave portions of those articles into this longer essay. I am also grateful to the colleagues and friends with whom I have discussed the problems of this essay, in particular Norman Maclean, William Veeder, Sheldon Sacks, Donald Scott, Jerome McGann, Charles Wegener, Edward Rosenheim, Jr., and Arthur Heiserman of the University of Chicago; Fred Jaher of the University of Illinois; Alexander C. Kern and Paul Baender of the University of Iowa, Morton Ross of the University of Edmonton, and Wilson O. Clough, Herbert Deitrich, Gene Gressley and Robert Hemenway of the University of Wyoming. Most of what I have understood of the psychoanalytic approach to literature, I have gained from conversations and correspondence with Harold Boris of Tufts University. Ray Browne of the Popular Press of Bowling Green State University has encouraged me enormously in the effort to get it all down. And finally I would like to thank my students at the University of Chicago and the University of Iowa and especially those of the Documentary Film Group of the University of Chicago whose help made it possible for me to deal with the Western films: above all Barbara Bernstein, who was my research assistant during the year I wrote this essay and who helped in innumerable ways not least in compiling the filmography which accompanies the essay; and those others with whom I had so many discussions about the Western: Charles Flynn, Terry Fox, Rick Thompson, Fred Stein, Myron Meisel and Jim Jubak. And special thanks to my student David P. James for designing the cover of this book.

University of Chicago   1970

Reflections on the Western Since 1970

THE SIX-GUN MYSTIQUE came into being by chance. In the early 1960s, I read an essay on the Western by my colleague Peter Homans. Though most interesting, Homans' essay made me think about the methods with which scholars had approached popular genres and led me to ruminate about alternative ways of looking at this American artistic and mythical phenomenon. Summoning up memories of a youth misspent in Saturday matinees, I plunged into the scholarly literature on the Western. I discovered that while there were a number of excellent essays about the Western from varying points of view, there was no one volume which had pulled these materials together. So I decided to edit an anthology of the best essays I could find. I thought I would begin with a brief introduction to display the wares. Once started, I found I could not stop. That brief introduction grew until it was too long for an anthology and too short for a book.

Not knowing quite what to do with this ungainly progeny, I spoke to Ray Browne, who, more than any other person has stimulated and encouraged studies in popular culture. Ray, with his usual flexibility and hospitality, suggested that we publish the essay together with bibliographies and filmographies as a guide to the study of the Western. Thus a brief introduction became *The Six-Gun Mystique.*

While far from a bestseller, *The Six-Gun Mystique* has continued to sell, and, I hope, be of some use to fellow students of the Western since its original publication in 1970.* I have particularly cherished the generous praise of Henry Nash

*It might amuse readers to know that the original publication of *SGM* was casual enough that we forgot to include a copyright date. Neither Ray nor I can remember whether it was 1970 or 1971, but have decided on 1970 to give it a greater air of antiquity.

1

Smith, whose *Virgin Land* so much inspired scholars to further studies in the mythology of the American West. I have also been pleased that many teachers of American Studies, popular culture and film have found the book useful as a text or supplementary reading.

Nearly fifteen years have passed since I completed *The Six-Gun Mystique*. During that time a great many changes have taken place in the scholarly study of the Western and in the Western genre itself. Ironically, scholarly and critical studies of the Western have flourished, while the Western as a vital popular genre has increasingly languished. Book after book, many of them outstanding in quality, have dealt with the mythology of the West. However, while I could point out in *The Six-Gun Mystique* that Western series dominated television in the late 1950s and 1960s, there has not been a successful new television Western in several years. During its high point as a film genre from around 1940-1960, as much as one fourth of the annual Hollywood output consisted of Westerns. In the 1980s, one successful Western film a year is about all one can expect. In this introduction to an introduction, I will explore both the burgeoning scholarly work about the Western and the reasons for its decline as a popular genre.

So much excellent writing and research about the West and the Western has been published since 1970 that it is difficult to avoid turning exposition into bibliography. For example, there have been several major synthetic histories of the West and the Westward movement, most notably the two crowning achievements of Ray Allen Billington and Frederick Merk, the old masters of Western history. Many particular histories have given us a better understanding of the development of the West. These histories have tended to counter the mythology of the West as regeneration through a sort of pastoral rebirth with an account of Western history as an episode in the advanced evolution of industrialism. Major works such as Allan Bogue's studies of Western agriculture have made it clear that land speculation and other patterns of advanced capitalism were far more important in the development of the West than the Lone Ranger.

One of the most important revisions in our view of the West brought about by the new Western history has been a basic change in our understanding of the relationship between the Western frontier and the rest of the country. The Turner thesis, which dominated the American historical imagination for much of the twentieth century, postulated the idea that the frontier experience was the true source of American democracy. The popular imagination in the nineteenth century had already reveled in the fantasy of the Wild West with its lawlessness and violent individualism. When combined with the Turner thesis, this fantasy made the frontier into the true source of violence in America, conveniently averting the public gaze from one of the most important causes of American violence—racism—and its true locus—the cities.

Not only has recent historical research raised many doubts about the Turner thesis, it has overwhelmingly demonstrated that the West was actually far less violent than the South and the Eastern cities. Richard Wade and his students have shown that Turner's view of the frontier experience as a recurrent reversion to pastoral simplicity is belied by the fact that cities were usually well established before the surrounding countryside and that Western cities played a crucial role in organizing and directing the peopling of the West. Robert Dykstra's studies of Kansas cattle towns has shown that the murder rate in Dodge City was surprisingly low, while Odie Faulk's *Tombstone* makes it clear that Wyatt Earp was hardly the good and gentle man whom Henry Fonda portrayed so wonderfully in *My Darling Clementine* and that the gunfight at the OK Corral was a much murkier episode than we had imagined. Studies in Western violence, including those commissioned by the President's Commission on the Causes and Prevention of Violence, show that there is a fundamental difference between the myths of Western violence and its actual incidence. As historian W. Eugene Hollen sums it up in his *Frontier Violence: Another Look* (1977) "the lawless aspect of Western frontier society has had a much greater appeal to the vicarious reader. Thus, a disproportionate amount of dramatic literature exists on violence in the West in comparison to the material available on the East." Hollen concludes that contrary to the traditional view that the Wild West was the center of violence in America, "frontier lawlessness was primarily the result, rather than the cause, of our violent society." (p. ix)

In addition to the social and political historians' increasing contributions to our knowledge of Western history, many more reliable treatments of Western writers have been written since 1970. For a long time, the study of writers whose inspiration largely derived from the West was a perennial stepchild of literary history. Fortunately, the trend in literary history away from a restrictive canon of literary greats toward a broader interest in many different kinds of literature and culture has helped stimulate the analysis of Western writers.*

This new attitude has encouraged scholars like John R. Milton, Don D. Walker, Delbert Wylder and Richard Etulain to study Western writers in depth. Many scholars have collaborated to produce a major reference work, *Fifty Western Writers* (1982) which reveals the variety and richness of Western writing.

Another sign of the growing awareness of the Western as a myth and a genre is the increasing use of Western materials by contemporary novelists who are not primarily concerned with the evocation of the traditional mythology. Thomas Berger's *Little Big Man* brilliantly uses both mythical and historical materials about the West to create a comic epic about the clash between Native Americans and Whites. Douglas Jones' *The Court Martial of George Armstrong Custer* probed the ambiguous realities of the Custer massacre in fictional form, while E.L. Doctorow's *Welcome to Hard Times* transformed the Western into a novel of the absurd. It is a particular pleasure to me that the man to whom the first edition of *The Six-Gun Mystique* was dedicated, Norman Maclean, has published *A River Runs Through It and Other Stories*, which has already become a Western classic of a very different sort than the usual story of regeneration through violence.

More careful studies of Western literature have been paralleled by attempts to trace the history and the significance of the Western film. A new edition of Fenin and Everson's basic

---

*Two important statements about the newer attitude toward culture are Herbert Gans, *Popular Culture and High Culture* and Leslie Fiedler, *What Was Literature?*

history of the Western film has brought their account close to the present, while Jon Tuska's *The Filming of the West* contains detailed information and anecdotes about the people who shaped the development of the genre. Books about Hollywood genres and studio history by Stuart Kaminsky, Thomas Schatz, Robert Sklar and Garth Jowett have greatly enriched our understanding of the Western genre in relation to other popular film formulas. The postwar Western and its reflection of changes in American culture and ideologies has been carefully analyzed in Philip French's *Westerns* and John Lenihan's *Showdown*. Several studies of individual films, directors and stars, such as Stuart Kaminsky's *Clint Eastwood* and *John Huston*, Paul Seydor's *Sam Peckinpah* and the interesting group of essays on individual Western films collected by William T. Pilkington and Don Graham, have given us a greater sense of the complexity and variety of the genre. Even the television Western has been carefully scrutinized in Ralph and Donna Brauer's *The Horse, the Gun and the Piece of Property* and in Horace Newcomb's *TV: The Most Popular Art*.

International interest in the Western has always been an important factor in the genre's popularity. In some ways, French, German, Italian and Japanese interest in the mythical forms of the Western has been stronger since 1970 than in America. In terms of analysis and criticism, the French have always been especially interesting with such important discussions as Andre Bazin's essays and Jean Rieupeyrout's analytical dictionary of Western iconography. A younger French intellectual, Jean-Louis Leutrat, has continued the French tradition with an excellent structural and aesthetic survey of the genre, *Le Western*. Both Rieupeyrout's earlier work and Leutrat's current book really should be translated into English and made more widely available for American students of popular culture.

To gain access to this new research in Western history and literature, we can be grateful to Richard Etulain for the excellent bibliographies and reference books he has edited with various collaborators, the afore-mentioned *Fifty Western Writers, Western American Literature* and *The Frontier and the American West*.

*   *   *

To analyze all the theoretical contributions to our
understanding of the Western genre in books and essays
published since *The Six-Gun Mystique* would be folly for an
introduction which is threatening like its predecessor to burst
the bounds of brevity and decorum. Fortunately, several good
anthologies such as Jack Nachbar's *Focus on the Western*
have completed the task of assembling basic essays on the
Western that *The Six-Gun Mystique* never accomplished.
These give a good idea of the range of interpretations the
Western genre has inspired. However, three books are of
particular importance. As I noted in the introduction to
Adventure, Mystery and Romance, the myth-symbol approach
which long dominated American studies has been one of the
most fruitful methodologies to be applied in the analysis of
popular genres. Most recently the methodologies and
ideologies of structuralism have become increasingly
influential on the students of popular culture.

Bruce Rosenberg's *Custer and the Epic of Defeat* is a very
effective synthesis of the traditional myth-symbol approach
and the new structuralism. It is extremely important not
only for the study of the Western but for any studies in
legend and mythology because it tells us a great deal about the
myth-making process. Centering his study around the Custer
massacre at the Little Big Horn in 1876, Rosenberg extends his
analysis to several traditional accounts of great defeats, such
as the defeat of Saul at Mt. Gilboa or that of Charlemagne's
rear guard as presented in the *Song of Roland.*By comparing
these various accounts of epic defeat, Rosenberg is able to show
that they have a remarkable number of characteristics in
common. For example, the heroic leader is always the last to
die. Then, by carefully comparing what we actually know
about the Battle of Little Big Horn with contemporary
newspaper accounts and later Custer biographies, Rosenberg
is able to show that even early accounts were closer to the
mythical archetype of epic defeat than to any known actuality.
Thus, Rosenberg shows that the myth-making process begins

immediately at the point where news of such an event is known to the world outside and is, consequently, an even more important human method of processing reality than was implied by the traditional thesis that myth-making grows as the reality recedes in time. Rosenberg offers several speculations about the reason why myth-making is so prevalent, including the structuralist notion that the human mind is best at storing binary structures. Hence, the dramatic oppositions of mythology are one of the best ways to store and process events. *Custer and the Epic of Defeat* is a work of major theoretical importance in the study of mythology and formulas and does a great deal to explain how and why people create and respond to archetypal patterns.

The most important book using the myth-symbol approach to the Western since *Virgin Land* is Richard Slotkin's *Regeneration Through Violence*. The idea of the Western as the embodiment of an archetypal pattern of redemptive and purgative violence is hardly new. As I pointed out in *The Six-Gun Mystique*, "the vision [of America as a redeemer nation] contrasted profoundly with the reality of an inordinately high level of individual and social aggression, beginning with the revolution which created the new nation and continuing through domestic and foreign wars of moralistic conquest and the violent subjugation of black people and Indians. To preserve the self-image it has been necessary to disguise the aggressive impulses in these historical realities under the mask of moral purity and social redemption through violence." In turn, I was influenced in this statement by Robert Warshow's essay on the Westerner and doubtless by many other critics of the Western who have made the same basic point.

However, Slotkin adds a new dimension to this generalization by the depth and complexity of his insights into particular works and by the range of his evidence. For one thing, Slotkin demonstrates that many of the mythical patterns important to the nineteenth and twentieth century Western originated not with Cooper in the early nineteenth century, but in the Captivity and Indian War narratives of the seventeenth and eighteenth centuries. In this way he indicates that the underlying themes of the Western are present in

America practically from the beginning of white settlement. His analysis also establishes very clearly the importance of racism and puritanism as ideological forces shaping the Western mythology. While there remain many questions about the myth-symbol approach as a methodology, Slotkin's work has certainly revitalized the concept of myth as a significant category of cultural analysis. Slotkin has recently published sequel to *Regeneration Through Violence* which brings analysis up to the twentieth century, showing how the myths that shaped the Western have also evolved into the American detective story or hard-boiled thriller. I will return to this later.

Another book which should have been of considerable theoretical interest but seemed ultimately disappointing to me was Will Wright's *Six-Guns and Society*. Two aspects of Wright's work were particularly important. First, he tried to define a clear principle of selection for those works which are to be considered the "text" of a popular genre for the purpose of cultural analysis. Wright chose his sample by using only those Westerns which showed the highest box-office grosses, figures which can be readily obtained by consulting entertainment industry periodicals like *Variety*. This is a perfectly reasonable way of defining the text of a popular genre for certain analytical purposes and it does avoid the arbitrariness often involved in analyses of thematic and structural changes in a genre. However, there are other kinds of problems in the study of popular genres which require different principles of selection. For example, if one is studying the influence of the Western on culture, or the way in which myths and ideologies shape the development of a genre in many different media or over a long period of time, one must inevitably use a broader range of material than the limited number of examples which have drawn the largest audiences. Furthermore, one always needs to be aware of the possibility that a very high popularity may reflect the influence of factors which are not necessarily a result of the genre itself, such as the public interest in certain film stars.

The most disappointing aspect of Wright's book lies in his attempt to apply a quasi-Marxian version of structuralist-functionalist analysis to account for the cultural significance of Western films. The methodology of structuralism has become extremely important in the study of language, literature and culture in the last two decades. Indeed, one thing I realized when I became more familiar with the ideas of structuralism after I wrote *The Six-Gun Mystique* was that like Moliere's M. Jourdain and prose, I had been doing structuralism all along. For structuralism is basically a highly systematized method of analyzing linguistic, literary and cultural formulas along with a body of theory about how to interpret the significance of these formulas. The analytical methods of the structuralists are well worth emulation and their concept of binary opposition as the basis of analysis has proved to be extraordinarily useful in the analysis of language and other cultural structures. The problem comes when we attempt to interpret the patterns which structuralist analysis defines. Such interpretations inevitably require further ideological assumptions and commitments and are, therefore, nearly as subjective as less systematic modes of analysis.

Wright makes an extremely dogmatic ideological commitment, which he doggedly carries through in his interpretations of the three different structural patterns he defines in the Western film. He is determined to show us that these patterns have a political function to express and reinforce the changing ideological conceptions of the bourgeoisie as it moves from earlier to later stages of capitalism. This rigidly politico-economic interpretation of the Western genre seems overly simplistic and reductionistic, because it fails to integrate the many factors that shape the development of a popular genre. One thing I did say in *The Six-Gun Mystique* which I still believe very strongly was that "a popular formula like the Western cannot be understood as the effect of any single factor .... Consequently, it is quite incorrect to think that the key to the Western's popularity lies in any particular social or psychological dynamic. Instead, the Western's capacity to accommodate many different kinds of meaning ... as well as its ability to respond to changing cultural themes and concerns—have made the formula successful as popular art and entertainment over many generations." In a later essay, "The Concept of Artistic Matrices," I tried to develop a systematic analysis of the several factors which shape the evolution of popular culture. I am sure that this treatment is still too simplistic, but it is, I believe, a definite improvement over the kind of reductionism which *Six-Guns and Society* fosters.

*   *   *

Perhaps the greatest change of all is that in 1970, I could still treat the Western as a flourishing popular genre, while in 1983, as I have indicated, the production of successful Westerns, particularly in film and for television is few and far between. I might have seen that this decline in the Western's hold over the public imagination was adumbrated in some important thematic changes in the major Westerns of the 1960s. It is no accident that, while earlier Westerns tended to deal with stories from the period of pioneering and the beginning of settlement, Westerns from the 1960s and 1970s dealt most powerfully with the end of the West, the passing of its heroic and mythical age and its entry into the modern world of cities and technology. In Sam Peckinpah's *Ride the High Country,* the aging heroes seem out of place in a world of policemen and automobiles. The climactic shootout is clearly one final apotheosis of the Code of the West. In *The Wild Bunch* aging bandits confront a modern world of machinery, militarism and social revolution which destroys them. The sense of the myth's archaism is even stronger in a recent film like *The Electric Horseman* where the protagonist is deeply concerned that he has become nothing more than a shadowy image of a ghostly past. The death of John Wayne, after a heroic battle against cancer, was widely felt to symbolize the end of an era, and in many ways it did. No younger actor has become a new avatar of the Western hero, and those who, like Clint Eastwood and Charles Bronson first became famous in spaghetti Westerns, have largely turned to other genres like the police saga and the spy thriller.

My guess is that the declining effectiveness of the Western as a popular genre results, in part, from the changing perception of the West itself. During the last part of the nineteenth century, the period when the Western really developed as a popular formula, the West was both a mythical landscape and an actual place. Readers of those dime novel adventures of cowboys, marshals and badmen could feel increased interest in these stories because they purported to be based on near contemporary events and characters. In other words, the Western conflated time and space so that the "old West" was a place of mysterious excitement and great deeds, but was also somehow present and real. As Mircea Eliade has taught us, one of the central characteristics of traditional myths is that they take place in a sacred time which is understood to be recurrently present, both in and out of history, both past and present. For a long period in the history of American culture, the West possessed these mysterious mythical qualities.

But in the years since 1970 the myth has become increasingly attenuated. For one thing, the West is becoming increasingly like the rest of the country, complete with standardized fast food franchises, shopping malls and housing developments which look much the same from New York City to Los Angeles. The increasing sameness of the West and the East has finally accomplished what Frederick Jackson Turner prophesied in 1893: the closing of the spatial frontier has led to the closing of a spiritual and cultural frontier. There is no more free land; only real estate values.

The increasing sameness of the West has been reinforced by a growing familiarity with Western places, customs and styles throughout the country and indeed throughout the world. When one can buy a package tour to ski in Colorado, to gamble in Las Vegas or to share the excitement of Frontier Days in Cheyenne, the result is tourism rather than adventure. When a businessman in New York City wears cowboy boots and a stetson, these articles of clothing rapidly lose their mythic iconicity and become just another outfit. When urban bars offer their patrons a mechanized bucking bronco and the rodeo is more spectacular in Madison Square Garden than in Montana, the Old West is truly long gone.

The geographic frontier of America is closed and is rapidly receding into the past. It seems to have been replaced in the public imagination by two new landscapes which possess some of the mythic power which was once associated with the Western frontier: the city and outer space. It is a critical cliche that movies like *Taxi-Driver* and *Star Wars* are urban and science fiction Westerns. But, though there is much truth in this, like any cliche, the observation is also very misleading. Outer space can, of course, be treated as a frontier, and like the West in an earlier time, it is both a mythical landscape and a contemporary actuality (cf. the mythmaking about the astronauts so effectively anatomized in Tom Wolfe's *The Right Stuff*). However, its qualities are different. For one thing, space adventure depends on a mastery of technology which requires a group effort and an interlocking between man and machine very different from the violent individualism of the classic Western. The great popular successes in science fiction adventure, such as the Star Trek and Star Wars series reflect very different values and styles from the pastoral and individualistic ambience of the Western. Even though the Western hero often had a side kick, this figure was generally either comic or of another race like the Lone Ranger's Tonto. Perhaps this survives to some extent in *Star Wars'* Wookee and *Star Trek*'s Mr. Spock, but these are far from comic or racial inferiors. Similarly, women play a much more active role as members of the heroic group than in the Western where heroic women tended to be either déclassé dance hall girls like Marlene Dietrich's Frenchy in *Destry Rides Again* or tomboys like Jean Arthur's Calamity Jane.

It's hard at first to understand how the city can be treated as a heroic frontier until one remembers that, in this suburban age, the inner city is a strange and frightening place associated primarily with increasing crime and violence by most middle-class white Americans. To these persons, the inner city is a dark and bloody ground, and it is comforting to imagine a lone individual hero acting out the Code of the West against gangsters, drug dealers, pimps and pornographers. In the long-running TV series *McCloud* Dennis Weaver, who once was a comic sidekick to *Gunsmoke's* Marshal Dillon, plays a Western lawman from Taos, New Mexico on temporary assignment to the New York City Police Department. McCloud ritually demonstrates that his Western individualism and cowboy skills are more effective against criminals than the organization and technology of his urban counterparts. *McCloud* can be very charming as a heroic fantasy but it depends on a good bit of tongue-in-cheek to make its adventures believable. Another sort of "urban Western" is represented by such films as *Midnight Cowboy, Taxi Driver, Prince of the City* and *The Godfather*, which are very unlike Westerns in their moral ambiguity and tragic complexity. In general, the urban frontier seems to call forth a more dubious kind of hero than the mythic Westerner. Clint Eastwood's Dirty Harry Callahan is obviously an urban avatar of some of his earlier Western heroes, but his ambiguous attitude toward law and order is inevitably made far more obvious a theme. Also, the "urban Western," like the science fiction adventure frequently requires a group and elaborate technology.

Some people argue that the spy thriller, another very popular contemporary genre, has much in common with the Western, but I think this observation really suggests that none of these genres are Westerns at all. They resemble the Western in that these genres are basically adventure stories. However, changing cultural attitudes have evoked new kinds of adventure and different types of hero to replace the traditional Westerner. This new kind of adventure story either represents a distant space-time in which monumental clashes between good and evil seem mythically appropriate or an immediate present with multiple ambiguities and more complex relations between heroes and villains. The few Westerns that have been made in the past decade have also reflected this uncertainty about values and the nature of heroism, but somehow the Western landscape with its starkly dramatic contrasts between town and wilderness, desert and mountains, does not seem as effective a background for such shifting and indeterminate meanings. The landscape of the modern city is more marked by spatial ambiguities which artistically reinforce the sense of moral and social ambiguity in the contemporary urban adventure and secret agent thriller.

Another factor that may have contributed to the decline of the Western is the increasing awareness writers, directors and producers have developed of the Western as a genre. I suggested in *Adventure, Mystery and Romance* that popular genres go through a cycle of development and decline. This cycle usually begins with a highly successful individual work which inspires many imitations and thus gives rise to a formula which serves as the basis of further developments. If the formula becomes important enough and remains so over a period of time, writers and other producers become increasingly self-conscious about what they are doing and come to understand the formula as a distinctive type or genre. At first, this awareness may produce the richest and best instances of the genre, but eventually the genre becomes more and more reflexive and begins to feed on itself through parodic and ironic versions of the type. When this happens a decline is almost certain to set in sooner or later, for the genre is no longer taken seriously by its creators.

Something like this has, I believe, happened to the Western. Beginning with the Leatherstocking Tales of James Fenimore Cooper, it became a formula in the multitudinous dime novels and early films of the late nineteenth and early twentieth centuries. Revitalized by the adult Western fiction of writers like Owen Wister, Emerson Hough and Harold Bell Wright, the Western film became a fully conscious genre in the late 1930s. The great Westerns created between 1940 and 1970 by directors like John Ford, Howard Hawks, Fred Zinneman, Anthony Mann, Budd Boetticher and Sam Peckinpah represent that classic phase of balance between awareness of the Western as a genre and commitment to the genre as a meaningful representation of life. The last director in this mold is Sam Peckinpah, whose central theme, the passing of the heroic time of the Old West, is also a way of expressing something about the exhaustion of the genre. After Peckinpah most successful Westerns have either been outright parodies of the genre like *Support Your Local Gunfighter* (1971), *The Life and Times of Judge Roy Bean* (1972), *Blazing Saddles* (1974) and *The Duchess and the Dirtwater Fox* (1976) or attempts to produce anti-Westerns which have the same moral ambiguities as the urban adventure or the modern spy story—*McCabe and Mrs. Miller* (1971), *Bad Company* (1972), *The Great Northfield Minnesota Raid* (1972), *Pat Garrett and Billy the Kid* (1973) *Buffalo Bill and the Indians* (1976), *The Missouri Breaks* (1976) and *Goin' South* (1978). The current predicament of the Western is encapsulated in Michael Cimino's ill-fated Western epic *Heaven's Gate* (1982). After his extraordinary success with *The Deer Hunter*, Cimino turned to the Western genre, evidently intending to make a major cinematic statement of what he viewed as *the* American myth. Even the title of *The Deer Hunter* resonated with echoes of James Fenimore Cooper (cf. *The Deerslayer*), while the story itself developed that mythical figure of the good hunter involved in the war between races into a powerfully titanic drama. Having, so to speak, done Cooper, Cimino became fascinated by the famous Western episode of the Johnson county war, which had served as the basis for Owen Wister's *The Virginian* and Jack Schaefer's *Shane*. However, Cimino tried to treat the conflict between ranchers and the farmers in terms of the contemporary themes that he had explored so effectively in *The Deer Hunter*: the traumatic impact of immigration on the immigrants, and the self-destructive violence of class and ethnic conflict. The result simply exploded the limited boundaries of the Western genre. In its initial version, reported to have lasted inordinately long, the film apparently both exasperated and exhausted its audience by its murky complexity and ambiguity. In the drastically cut version released to theaters and shown on cable television, the film was still profoundly puzzling, particularly if one brought to it the traditional expectation of dramatic and symbolic clarity, associated with the Western genre.

There appears to be one major source of the moral ambiguity so characteristic of popular genres since the early 1970s: the development of new and conflicting attitudes toward violence, sexism and racism as aspects of American culture. Not that our culture places any less emphasis on violence. The currently popular horror movies with their nauseatingly graphic portrayals of all sorts of gore are clear indications that Americans are still obsessed with violence. The difference lies in the attitudes of people toward it. In the traditional Western a very strong distinction was made between good violence (perpetrated by the hero) and bad violence (that used by the villains in pursuit of their evil aims). Moreover, the hero was usually portrayed as very reluctant to enter into violence. Of course, once he did, his skill in the shootout was glorified as not only an appropriate punishment for the villain but as the apotheosis of the hero's unique identity. In the end the hero's violence seemed graceful, aesthetic and, even, fun.

However, in a society so forcibly aware of the actual horrors of violence in Vietnam and the Middle East, and of the rate of violent crime in America itself, violence portrayed as graceful or fun rings very hollow. One movie of the late 1960s, Arthur Penn's *Bonnie and Clyde*, powerfully presented this transformation within the context of the film's plot. At the beginning, the Barrow gang's violence seems like farcical highjinks, but Clyde's brutal and accidental murder of a bank teller shatters the sense of fun. By the time the movie reaches a final shootout in which Bonnie and Clyde are riddled with bullets by a sheriff's posse, violence has come to mean a force which, once unleashed, destroys the innocent along with the guilty. The Western hero's reluctance to initiate violence, and his "grace under pressure" seem archaic in an age of mass terror and potential nuclear catastrophe. Many people who saw the television movie *The Day After* reported feeling disappointed because its portrayal of nuclear holocaust was not violent or "gory" enough. Such reactions may seem terribly callous until one realizes that young people have grown up in a world of escalating terrorism and atomic horror in which the individual feels vulnerable to violent attack at any moment. In such a world, the relatively orderly rituals of violence characteristic of the traditional Western seem sanitized and pale. Yet, to increase the level, the randomness and the ambiguity of violence in the Western destroys one of its major themes: that there is a kind of redemption, or to use Richard Slotkin's phrase, a regeneration through violence, when it is appropriately applied by the heroic individual.

Another source of ambiguity which the Western genre has found it difficult to integrate is the contemporary concern with sexuality, both in the sense of sexual roles and of sex itself. It embarrases me that even though I adapted the title of *The Six-Gun Mystique* from Betty Friedan's feminist work *The Feminine Mystique*, I made so few significant comments on the role of sex and sexism in the Western. Looking back over the original text, it seems to consist, in this area, mainly of truisms, such as that the Western hero is less interested in women than most mythical protagonists, and that the genre was primarily masculine in its orientation. In the years since the publication of *The Six-Gun Mystique*, I, like many other males of my generation, have become increasingly aware of the role of sexism in American life. Through this heightened awareness, I think I have come to understand more fully how sexism has shaped the tradition of the Western. Basically, the Western genre, throughout most of its history . . . , has played down the importance of sex and of women in a man's life by the simple device of making love a reward for heroism rather than a continual part of life. The hero must clean up the town before he can settle down with his woman, if then. One of the memorable scenes which ends so many Westerns is that of the hero promising to return and marry the heroine. In Mel Brooks' *Blazing Saddles*, this conventional scene is burlesqued by having the hero ride off into the sunset with another man! Though the evidence is not fully clear on the point, there is some indication that homosexuality was quite rampant in the Old West, but this is a theme that the Western has not been able to accommodate. Better to portray the hero as a near-virgin than as a flaming homosexual.

Another aspect of sexism in the traditional Western was pointed out long ago by Henry Nash Smith in *Virgin Land* and further developed by Leslie Fiedler in *Love and Death in the American Novel*. This was the archetypal contrast between virginal blond and sexier but tainted brunette so typical of nineteenth century melodrama. It entered the Western with Cooper's characters Alice and Cora Munro in *The Last of the Mohicans* and, transmuted into the dialectic between the Eastern school marm and the dance hall girl, it has been almost as stable a feature of the Western formula as the horse and the gun. Of course there has been considerable change in the value ascribed to these two archetypal women. Cooper found it necessary to kill Cora off before she could mate with Uncas, the Mohican, but in the middle decades of the twentieth century, the dance-hall girl has been increasingly appreciated from Marlene Dietrich's wonderful portrayal of Frenchie in *Destry Rides Again* to Amanda Blake's Miss Kitty of the Long Branch saloon (*Gunsmoke*) and Marilyn Monroe's performance as a blonde dance hall girl in Arthur Miller and John Huston's *The Misfits*. There was also Joan Crawford's striking role as the female protagonist of Nicholas Ray's *Johnny Guitar* complete with designer-made cowboy outfit and a six-gun. While one can construe this tendency as a gradual decrease of sexism, certain other aspects of the development of the Western genre in the same period suggest that we should at least qualify the notion of a gradually eroding sexism in the genre.

For one thing, the schoolmarm-dancehall girl antithesis still lurked at the heart of the genre and was embodied in many of the most successful Westerns of the mid-twentieth century. Let me note here just two instances, one is a film generally acknowledged to be one of the truly great Westerns of the forties and the other, of the fifties.

In John Ford's *My Darling Clementine* the schoolmarm is actually a nurse who has come to Tombstone from the East to find Doc Holiday, formerly her fiance. However, for reasons none too clear, Doc has turned his back on the East and all it represents to become a gambler and saloon owner in Tombstone. He has also become sexually involved with Chihauhua, a half-breed girl who hangs around his saloon. This girl, jealous at what she believes to be Doc's interest in nurse Clementine, falsely accuses him as a murderer to Wyatt Earp is herself shot by another of her lovers and dies. In the meantime, Wyatt Earp has fallen in love with Clementine, whom he leaves behind in Tombstone as he continues his quest, with a promise to return someday. Clementine, of course, is staying in Tombstone to take up schoolteaching.

The second instance is *High Noon*. In this movie aging Marshal Gary Cooper has recently married the chastely blond and cultivated Grace Kelly, who wants her husband to give up his dangerous and violent job. Before he can do so, news arrives that a vicious murderer who hates the marshal has been released from prison and will arrive in town on the noon train to join his gang of killers in avenging himself. The marshal seeks help from the townspeople but is refused. He finally visits sensuously brunette Katy Jurado, a dancehall girl with whom he has had a long standing affair. Jurado offers to help him if he will leave his wife. The marshal refuses her offer and goes off to face the killers alone. In the end, with a change of heart similar to that of Molly Stark in *The Virginian*,

Kelly shoots the last remaining killer in the back before he is able to shoot her husband.

Film critic Molly Haskell has also suggested another sexist tendency in Westerns of the fifties and sixties. Her book, *From Reverence to Rape*, describes a new kind of film which she calls the "buddy movie." In this type of movie, the relationship between men is far more important than any encounters between men and women. It is true that in Westerns like *Butch Cassidy and the Sundance Kid, The Wild Bunch* and *The Professionals* women and sex are pushed into the background. Whatever complex feelings exist in these movies grow out of male friendship. Haskell thinks that the flourishing of such films in recent times reflects a male backlash on the part of creators and audiences against women's demands for equality and independence.

Whether Haskell's interpretation of the motivations behind the recent rash of buddy movies is correct, it is certainly accurate that a strong emphasis on male bonding has always been an important tendency in the Western. As Leslie Fiedler pointed out in 1948, the drama of male comradeship has always been a basic theme of American literature from Hawkeye and Chingachgook through Ishmael and Queequeg, Huck Finn and Nigger Jim, The Lone Ranger and Tonto, down to today's Hawkeye Pierce and Trapper John. Fiedler even suggests that this theme traditionally reflected the desire of American males to escape from the civilizing and moralizing restraints of women. The frequently double edged portrayal of the schoolmarm in the Western represents a gentility toward which the hero aspires along with a limitation on his actions which he fears. This suggests that there is something to Fiedler's interpretation. In *The Virginian*, the hero finally had to tell his schoolmarm sweetheart that "a man's got to do what a man's got to do." John Ford makes a similar point in *Stagecoach* when he has the "Ladies Law and Order League" expel from town the only free spirits in it: a dancehall girl (prostitute) with a heart of gold and a drunken doctor. Thus, despite some surface changes the Western genre has always had a basically sexist orientation, and this, too, makes it difficult to create an effective contemporary Western. Of course our culture has not gone very far in eliminating sexism.

However, no one wants to make an expensive movie which runs the risk of alienating half its potential audience. Yet a Western without sexism doesn't seem like a Western. One of the recent attempts to make a television series with a Western setting came up with the idea of making a schoolmarm the protagonist. It quickly flopped.

Finally, a new awareness of the centrality of racism to American culture is a third moral ambiguity that has made the traditional formula no longer acceptable. Long before the publication of *The Six-Gun Mystique* historians like Philip Durham and Everett Jones were trying to change the lily-white Anglo-Saxon version of Western mythology by pointing out how important Blacks and Latinos were in the development of the West. In additon, generations of dedicated anthropologists have studied the many cultures of the Native American and have tried to inform the public of the actual richness of these cultures in contrast to the simplistic versions of noble and violent savages which continued to dominate the mythology of the West. What was most importantly lacking was a perception of Native Americans, Blacks and Latinos as something other than pathetic victims or evil resisters of the advance of White pioneers.

In the 1970s both events and new kinds of publications had a considerable impact on the consciousness of the White public. Most importantly Blacks, Latinos and Native Americans developed their own spokespersons and perspectives about the history of American culture. The emergent Black and Latino consciousnesses have changed our awareness of many aspects of American culture as well as the Western. The self-awareness of Native Americans has been particularly significant in our perception of Western history and myth. The public has been made much more aware of the Native American perspective through an outstanding group of writings by Native Americans and by those concerned with criticizing the White mythology of Western history. Indian essayists and fiction writers like Vine Deloria, N. Scott Momaday and Leslie Silko, White historians like Alvin Josephy and Dee Brown, whose *Bury My Heart at Wounded Knee* (1971) was a striking bestseller, presented the history of the West from a Native American point of view, while reprinted masterpieces like John

G. Neihardt's *Black Elk Speaks* and the Native American photographs of Edward Curtis, gave a new dimension and complexity to our understanding of the West. Many of these threads came together in a brilliant analysis and criticism of White attitudes toward the Indian, Robert Berkhofer's *The White Man's Indian* (1978) which, among other things, traced the process and the motives which transformed the Native American from a human being into a myth. It seems clear that our changed understanding of the Native American makes it increasingly difficult to treat Indians in the traditional Western fashion as savage antagonists or faithful companions. Films like *The Searchers, Cheyenne Autumn, Little Big Man, Soldier Blue, Ulzana's Raid* and even *Billy Jack* and *Winterhawk* testify to the importance of changing concepts of the Native American as an aspect of the mythology of the West.

The future, then, seems quite dim for anything resembling the traditional Western formula. Yet, the cinematic possibilities of the genre and its rich catalog of legendary characters and situations continue to attract writers and film and television directors and producers. One of the big bestsellers of the bicentennial year was James Michener's *Centennial* (from which one is tempted to say, with all due respect to Mr. Michener's great gifts, the Western may never recover). Actually, what Michener's version of the West showed was how effectively elements of the traditional Western could be combined with other aspects of the contemporary bestseller to create a new kind of Western. The one enormously successful contemporary Western writer, Louis L'Amour, has discovered this new synthesis in his own way and has used it to achieve nearly the same popularity that Zane Grey attained in the 1920s. L'Amour's continuing success has also inspired a new collaborative series, *Wagons West*, a carefully planned paperback series which has also achieved large sales. However, the success of these new style Westerns may be related to the degree to which they have left the traditional Western behind.

Will the Western ever experience a resurgence in popularity and regain its centrality as the American popular genre? If the reflections I have offered are largely correct, that seems unlikely. However, in closing, I would like to say to my many friends (especially Ray Merlock) who are diehard Western fans that I would not be terribly surprised and certainly delighted should it turn out that I am wrong. It may be that the eclipse of the Western I have described is only a temporary state and not a permanent decline. After all, the Western had degenerated into the simplicities of the dime novel when it was revitalized at the end of the nineteenth century by writers like Owen Wister, Emerson Hough and Harold Bell Wright, and by the development of the Western film. Then, after a dearth of Western films in the 1930s, the genre exploded into its golden age in the 1940s and 1950s. Even the Lone Ranger has recently ridden again, though not very successfully. Yet, let us not give up hope that we may hear, sometime again, out of the past, the thundering hoofbeats of the great horse Silver.

University of Kentucky   1984

Selected Bibliography Since 1970

A. *Books About the West and Western Mythology.*

Berkhofer, Robert F. Jr., *The White Man's Indian* (New York: Knopf, 1978).

Billington, Ray A. *Westward Expansion: A History of the American Frontier.* 4th ed. (New York, 1974).

Brown, Dee. *Bury My Heart at Wounded Knee: An Indian History of the American West* (New York: Holt, Rinehart and Winston, 1971).

Cawelti, John G. *Adventure, Mystery and Romance* (Chicago: University of Chicago Press, 1976).

Cawelti, John G. "God's Country, Las Vegas, and the Gunfighter." *The American West* Vol. 9 no. 4 273-283.

Cawelti, John G. "The Gunfighter and Society." *The American West*, 5 no. 2 (March 1968), 30-35.

Cawelti, John G. "Images of the Frontier and the Native American." In Joshua C. Taylor, *America as Art* (Washington: Smithsonian Institution, 1976).

Cawelti, John G. "Myths of Violence in American Popular Culture." *Critical Inquiry*, Vol. 1 no. 3 (Spring 1975).

Cawelti, John G. "The Okie, the Gunfighter and the Prophet." In *The Great Plains Experience*, ed. Gressley and Socolofsky (National Endowment for the Humanities, 1975).

Cawelti, John G. "Prolegomena to the Western." *Western American Literature*, Vol. 4 no. 4 (Winter 1970), 259-271.

Cawelti, John G. "Photographing the Western Sublime." in Joel Snyder and Doug Munson, *The Documentary Photograph as a Work of Art.* (David and Alfred Smart Gallery, University of Chicago, 1976) pp. 25-30.

Cawelti, John G., "Shifting Narrative Structures in a Changing American Culture," in Sam Girgus (ed.) *Myth, Popular Culture and the American Experience* (Albuquerque: University of New Mexico Press, 1980).

Cawelti, John G. "Trends in Recent American Genre Fiction." *Kansas Quarterly* (1978).

Cawelti, John G. "Zane Grey and W.S. Hart: The Romantic Western of the 1920s." *The Velvet Light Trap* 12 (Spring 1974), 7-10.

Deloria, Vine, Jr. *God is Red* (New York: Grosset and

Dunlap, 1973).

Etulain, Richard W. and Fred Erisman (eds.). *Fifty Western Writers* (Westport, CT: Greenwood Press, 1982).

Etulain. Richard W. and Rodman W. Paul. *The Frontier and the American West*, Goldentree Bibliographies (Arlington Heights, IL: AHM Publishing Co., 1977).

Etulain, Richard W. *Western American Literature: A Bibliography of Interpretive Books and Articles* (Vermillion, S.D.: Dakota Press, 1972).

Fender, Stephen. *Plotting the Golden West: American Literature and the Rhetoric of the California Trail.* (Cambridge: Cambridge University Press, 1981).

Graham, Hugh Davis and Ted Robert Gurr, (eds.) *Violence in America: Historical and Comparative Perspectives* (New York: New American Library, 1969).

Hollon, W. Eugene. *Frontier Violence: Another Look* (New York: Oxford, 1974).

Katz, William Loren. *The Black West* (Garden City, N.Y.: Doubleday, 1971).

Merk, Frederick. *History of the Westward Movement.* (New York: Knopf, 1978).

Rosenberg, Bruce. *Custer and the Epic of Defeat* (State College, PA: Pennsylvania State University Press, 1974).

Schlissel, Lillian. *Women's Diaries of the Westward Movement* (New York: Schocken Books, 1982).

Slotkin, Richard. *Regeneration Through Violence: The Mythology of the American Frontier, 1600-1860* (Middletown: CT: Wesleyan Univ. Press, 1973).

B. Books About the Western Film Genre

Adams, Les and Buck Rainey. *Shoot-Em-Ups: The Complete Reference Guide to Westerns of the Sound Era* (New Rochelle, N.Y.: Arlington House, 1978).

Brauer, Ralph and Donna. *The Horse, The Gun and the Piece of Property: Changing Images of the TV Western* (Bowling Green: The Popular Press, 1975).

Brownlow, Kevin. *The War, The West, and the Wilderness* (New York: Knopf, 1979).

Calder, Jenni. *There Must be a Lone Ranger: The*

American West in Film and Reality (New York: McGraw-Hill, 1974).

Etulain, Richard, ed., *Journal of the West*,22:4 (Oct. 1983). Special issue on Western films.

Eyles, Allen. *The Western* (New York: Barnes, 1975).

Fenin, George N. and William K. Everson. *The Western: From Silents to the Seventies* (New York: Grossman, 1973). Revised ed. of *The Western: From Silents to Cinerama (1962).*

Frayling, Christopher. *Spaghetti Westerns* (London: Routledge and Kegan Paul, Ltd., 1981).

French, Philip. *Westerns: Aspects of a Movie Genre* (New York: Viking, 1973).

Friar, Ralph and Natasha. *The Only Good Indian* (New York: Drama Book Specialists,1972).

Garfield, Brian. *Western Films: A Complete Guide* (New York: Rawson Associates, 1982).

Grant, Barry K. ed. *Film Genre, Theory and Criticism* (Metuchen, N.J.: Scarecrow Press, 1977).

Horwits, James. *They Went Thataway* (New York: Dutton, 1976).

Kaminsky, Stuart M. *American Film Genres: Approaches to a Critical Theory of Popular Film* (Dayton, O.: Pflaum, 1974).

Koszarski, Diane K. *The Complete Films of William S. Hart, A Pictorial Record* (New York: Dover, 1980).

Lenihan, John H. *Showdown: Confronting Modern America in the Western Film* (Urbana: Univ. of Illinois Press, 1980).

Leutrat, Jean-Louis, *Le Western* (Paris: Armand Colin, 1973).

Meyer, William R. *The Making of the Great Westerns* (New Rochelle, N.Y.: Arlington House, 1979).

Miller, Don. *Hollywood Corral* (New York: Popular Library, 1976).

Nachbar, Jack, ed. *Focus on the Western* (Englewood Cliffs, N.J.: Prentice-Hall, 1974).

Nachbar, Jack. *Western Films: An Annotated Critical Bibliography* (New York: Garland, 1975).

Schatz, Thomas. *Hollywood Genres: Formulas, Filmmaking, and the Studio System* (Philadelphia: Temple University Press, 1981).

Pilkington, William T. and Don Graham, eds. *Western Movies* (Albuquerque, N.M.: University of New Mexico Press, 1979).

Rothel, David. *The Singing Cowboys* (New York: Barnes, 1978).

Seydor, Paul. *Peckinpah: The Western Films* (Urbana: University of Illinois Press, 1980).

Solomon, Stanley, J. *Beyond Formula: American Film Genres* (New York: Harcourt, 1976).

Tatum, Stephen, "The Western Film Critic as 'Shootist' " *The Journal of Popular Film and Television*, 11 (Fall 1983), No. 3 114-121.

Note: I didn't encounter this very witty article until I had nearly completed the first draft of this introduction. I don't think Mr. Tatum and I differ greatly in our assessment of the situation, though we have different ideas about causes.

Tuska, Jon. *The Filming of the West* (Garden City, N.Y.: Doubleday, 1976).

Wright, Will. *Six Guns and Society: A Structural Study of the Western* (Berkeley: University of California Press, 1975).

C. *Works of fiction and poetry which employ Western materials and themes.*

Jones, Douglas C. *The Court-Martial of George Armstrong Custer* (New York: Scribner's, 1976).

Berger, Thomas. *Little Big Man* (New York: Dial, 1964).

Hill, Ruth Beebe. *Hanta Yo* (Garden City, N.Y.: Doubleday, 1979).

Maclean, Norman. *A River Runs Through It and Other Stories* (Chicago: University of Chicago Press, 1976).

Mailer, Norman. *The Executioner's Song* (Boston: Little, Brown, 1979).

Michelson, Peter, *Pacific Plainsong I-XIII* (Boulder, Colorado: Brilling Works, 1978).

Michener, James A., *Centennial* (New York: Random House, 1974).

Warren, Robert Penn, *Chief Joseph of the Nez Perce* (New York: Random House, 1982).

Selected Filmography

1970	*The Ballad of Cable Hogue* Sam Peckinpah
1970	*Little Big Man* Arthur Penn
1970	*The Cheyenne Social Club* Gene Kelly
1970	*Rio Lobo* John Hawks
1970	*A Man Called Horse* Elliot Silverstein
1970	*Monte Walsh* William A. Fraker
1970	*Tell Them Willie Boy Is Here* Abraham Polonsky
1970	*Soldier Blue* Ralph Nelson
1970	*Two Mules for Sister Sara* Donald Siegel
1971	*Big Jake* George Sherman
1971	*Doc* Frank Perry
1971	*The Hired Hand* Peter Fonda
1971	*Lawman* Michael Winner
1971	*McCabe and Mrs. Miller* Robert Altman
1971	*Red Sun* Terence Young
1971	*Shoot Out* Henry Hathaway
1971	*Support Your Local Gunfighter* Burt Kennedy
1971	*Valdez is Coming* Edwin Sherin
1972	*Bad Company* Robert Benton
1972	*Buck and the Preacher* Sidney Poitier
1972	*Chato's Land* Michael Winner
1972	*The Cowboys* Mark Rydell
1972	*The Culpepper Cattle Co.* Dick Richards
1973	*The Great Northfield Minnesota Raid* Philip Kaufman
1972	*Hannie Caulder* Burt Kennedy
1972	*Jeremiah Johnson* Sydney Pollack
1972	*Junior Bonner* Sam Peckinpah
1972	*The Life and Times of Judge Roy Bean* John Huston
1972	*They Call Me Trinity* E.B. Clucher
1972	*Ulzana's Raid* Robert Aldrich
1972	*When the Legends Die* Stuart Millar

1973   *Dirty Little Billy* Stan Dragoti
1973   *High Plains Drifter* Clint Eastwood
1973   *The Man Who Loved Cat Dancing* Richard C. Sarafian
1973   *Pat Garrett and Billy the Kid* Sam Peckinpah
1974   *Blazing Saddles* Mel Brooks
1974   *My Name is Nobody* Tinino Valerii
1975   *Bite the Bullet* Richard Brooks
1975   *Breakheart Pass* Tom Gries
1975   *Hearts of the West* Howard Zieff
1975   *Posse* Kirk Douglas
1975   *Rooster Cogburn* Stuart Millar
1976   *Buffalo Bill and the Indians: Or Sitting Bull's History Lesson* Robert Altman
1976   *The Duchess and the Dirtwater Fox* Melvin Frank
1976   *Great Scout and Cathouse Thursday* Don Taylor
1976   *Missouri Breaks* Arthur Penn
1976   *The Outlaw Josey Wales* Clint Eastwood
1976   *The Return of a Man Called Horse* Irvin Kershner
1976   *The Shootist* Don Siegel
1977   *Grayeagle* Charles B. Pierce
1977   *The White Buffalo* J. Lee Thompson
1978   *Comes A Horseman* Alan Pakula
1978   *Goin' South* Jack Nicholson
1978   *The Electric Horseman* Sidney Pollack
1980   *Heavens' Gate* Michael Cimino
1980   *Bronco Billy* Clint Eastwood
1982   *The Man From Snowy River* George Miller
1982   *Barbarosa* Fred Schespci

The Six-Gun Mystique

MANY OF MY GENERATION probably remember bolting dinner and rushing to the radio to hear the opening bars of Rossini's *William Tell Overture* followed by the thundering hoofbeats of the great horse Silver. Three times a week, year in and year out, the Lone Ranger rode the radio networks from station WXYZ in Detroit. Those of us who were true addicts came to know every conceivable regularity and variation within the half-hour program format. To this day, though it has been some 20 years since I last heard the great cry "Hi-ho Silver," I can still remember the shape of the program. I believe I could state almost to a minute the time that elapsed between the opening and the first gunshot, a time that varied little from year to year. In fact, during the several years of my regular listening to the masked man's exploits, I can remember few exceptions in the basic pattern of the program. Everything was precisely worked out from the opening introduction to the last dying away of the Lone Ranger's voice as he, Silver and Tonto rode away after bringing law and justice into the life of still another western community. Even a change in commercials became a noticeable and almost disturbing event in this grand stylized parade from beginning, through middle, to end. As I recall my responses to this peculiar work of art, it seems perfectly clear that the compelling thing about it was not so much the particular content of any of the episodes—I have long since forgotten what happened on any particular program and doubt that I even paid much attention to it at the time—but the vigorous clarity and the dynamic but somehow reassuring regularity of the form itself.

I was certainly not alone in my enthusiasm for the Western. Surely no twentieth century American needs to have the Western's importance as a cultural form demonstrated to him. Uncountable Westerns mark the course of American

29

history. At first glance, they seem as numerous as the sands of the desert. To get some statistical picture of the form's significance, let us take the period of the late 1950s. Expressed in terms of numbers of booktitles published, Westerns constituted 10.76% of the works of fiction published in 1958 and 1.76% of all books published. In 1959 eight of the top ten shows on television, as measured by Neilsen ratings, were Westerns and thirty of the prime-time shows were horse operas. At least 54 Western feature films were made in 1958. Some falling off in quantity and in popularity has occurred since the late 1950s, but the Western still occupies a unique place. In 1967, Westerns constituted 7.08% of published works of fiction and .74% of the total book production. During a typical week of TV (Saturday, September 16, to Friday, September 22, 1967) eighteen hours of Westerns were screened on Chicago's four major stations between the hours of six and ten in the evening, comprising approximately 16% of the total viewing time. And, in the same year Hollywood turned out approximately 37 major Western features. A sampling of further statistics indicates the continual popularity of the Western throughout the twentieth century. The modern Western apparently began with Owen Wister's novel *The Virginian*. A best-seller in 1902-03, this novel has accumulated total sales of 1,736,299. Zane Grey, Wister's successor as the most popular author of Westerns, occupied the best-seller lists continuously from 1917-1925. His books have accumulated a total sale of over 40 million copies. Jack Schaefer's *Shane* (1954), the most popular of recent Westerns, has sold nearly two million copies in the fifteen years since its publication. The Western movie has been a basic commodity of the American film industry since 1903, when Porter's "The Great Train Robbery" demonstrated its immense potential for exciting cinematic action. Hundreds of Western movies were turned out during the silent era by such stars as Bronco Billy Anderson, Tom Mix, and William S. Hart, and from the early thirties to the early sixties, the production of major Western features rarely fell below 50 each year.

There are probably some quantitative trends in Western production during the twentieth century, but I cannot pin them down with any certainty because of the Western's shift from one medium to another. For example, during the thirties and forties the pulp Western magazine was a major industry. In 1945, 30 Western adventure pulps and 6 Western love magazines were published regularly. By 1968 this number had fallen off precipitously to 9 Western magazines, many of which specialized in popular history rather than in romantic adventure. However, to conclude that this figure represents a decline in the popularity of the Western would clearly be wrong, because of the way in which TV has taken over the role of the pulp magazines. Similarly the decline in the production of Westerns since the beginning of the 1960s may be only a temporary pause. Though the proportion of Western feature films has fallen off in the last few years, the number of Western feature films has begun to rise again after a low of about 11 in 1962-63. The international Western, in particular the Clint Eastwood films made in Italy and Spain and directed by Italian Sergio Leone, has brought about a significant resurgence in popularity of the Western film, and in 1967 production was up to 37 again.

Because it is such a widely popular form, the Western has attracted attention from psychologists, sociologists and historians as well as from critics of the film. The studies of these specialists from different disciplines give us a unique opportunity to survey various methods of interpreting the relation between works of art, the society which produces them and the psychological dynamics which they reflect. In addition, the scholarly literature on the Western poses the problem of whether the different disciplines of the humanities and the social and psychological sciences can make use of each other's methods and findings. Can the conclusions of the literary critic and the psychoanalyst, the historian and the sociologist be synthesized in such a way that they illuminate one another's interpretation of art and culture? Or are the separate disciplines so different that they cannot effectively exchange their insights or relate them to a single system of explanation? In this essay, I will attempt to canvass some of the central difficulties and possibilities in the interdisciplinary interpretation of popular artistic forms, using the Western as my primary example.

I

In the first flush of enthusiasm over the great nineteenth century developments in sociology, psychology and naturalistic philosophy, many students of literature and art began to interpret all works in terms of some principle of social or psychological determinism. Gradually three major forms of deterministic interpretation developed. The first, exemplified in Hippolyte Taine's axiom that literature is determined by race, moment and milieu, assumes simply that literature is best understood as a reflection of the dominant intellectual and political concerns of a period, and of the special and unique characteristics of a race or culture. Though the racial determinism which was so popular in the late nineteenth and early twentieth centuries has largely gone out of fashion at least as far as modern European and American literature is concerned, the concept of unique national cultures still plays a major role in literary analysis. A number of essays interpret the Western as an expression of certain unique problems or aspects of the American experience. The primary interpretive method used in these essays is the discussion of social and political themes. For example, many critics of the Western interpret it as a representation of the theme of individualism. As Martin Nussbaum puts it, the Western hero is "a vanishing symbol of individualism in an age of togetherness and conformity."[1] Frederick Elkin suggests that "another group of values emphasized in the Western are derived more directly from frontier history and suggest that America has a rich and exciting heritage. These values focus on rugged individualism, frontier folk equality, and other characteristics of the Western way of life."[2] This method of theme-gathering is a simple and fruitful one and will probably continue to be of great use in the analysis of literature. Unfortunately, it possesses three major shortcomings.

First, the concept of theme is extremely vague, for any element of a work can serve as a theme. In the case of the Western, critics have pointed out a remarkable variety of themes, ranging from the Oedipus conflict, through individualism, to such motifs as innocence, primitivism and racism. No doubt most of these things are important in some way as reflections of culture or epoch, but the concept of theme fails to provide us with any way of determining which themes are more important than others or even how one theme is related to another. It merely postulates that any element in the work which appears to relate to some aspect of the culture is a reflection of that culture. This becomes particularly problematic when we encounter themes or motifs which seem to contradict each other in the same work. For example, the Western commonly presents the pioneer as a good figure and seemingly reflects approval of the concept or theme of progress. At the same time, many Westerns suggest a basic incompatibility between heroic figures like the marshal and the gunfighter and the social order being created by progress. Are we to say then that the theme of the Western is progress or anti-progress? Or both? How do we account for conflicting themes or values? Already these questions suggest that the simple equation of an element in a work of art with some cultural idea of value requires further elaboration. Indeed, some critics have suggested ways of accounting for the presence of conflicting values in works of art. For example, there is the theory of overt or explicit and latent values which suggests that one of the functions of art is to express conflicts of social value and thereby to harmonize or reconcile what might otherwise be perceived as disruptive forces in the culture. But such ideas already take us far beyond the simple conception of the Western as a reflection of major cultural themes.

The second difficulty with the method of theme analysis is the way in which it encourages us to take elements out of context and therefore to interpret not a total work, but a random collection of isolated elements. While I am not prepared to demonstrate the proposition with hard psychological evidence, it seems axiomatic to me that we experience works of narrative or drama like the Western as wholes and that we understand individual elements by virtue of their relation to a total structure of action, character and thought. In other words, a hero in a Western is a hero because he does certain kinds of things to certain types of people and we do not understand his heroism except in relation to the whole pattern of action. Similarly, a theme like individualism is defined not in isolation, but in connection with a complex pattern of values. Insofar as this is true, our attempts to interpret the Western or any other narrative or dramatic work by concentrating our attention on a certain number of themes is bound to result in a distortion of that work.

This kind of distortion leads to a third weakness in the conception of thematic analysis. The analysis of works as direct reflections of social or cultural themes commonly leads to a simple equation between the experience of works of art and other kinds of experience. Thus, if we simply argue that certain incidents or characters in the Western are expressions of the American value of individualism, we are assuming that our experience of these incidents in a narrative or dramatic work is no different from our experience of such incidents in an ordinary social context. But if anything is clear about our experience of narrative or dramatic works it is that it is not the same as our experience of life itself. Marshall McLuhan cites an incident where an African tribe viewing a movie on health ran in terror when a closeup of an insect appeared on the screen, apparently in the belief that some new kind of horrible monster was about to attack them. Clearly this group had not yet come to define the movies as something different from reality. Very few viewers of Western films make this mistake. I recall rather vividly the ending of Sam Peckinpah's recent Western *The Wild Bunch*. It was a terrible orgy of violence with bullets flying everywhere and blood and gore oozing from every pore, yet no person in the audience ducked or manifested any signs of horror or revulsion. Everyone understood this to be a movie and not life. Works of art do undoubtedly reflect social and cultural values, but we must consider this relationship in more complex terms than those suggested by the traditional method of analyzing and isolating social themes. Above all, our method must take into consideration two central aspects of works of art: a) that works of art are experienced as something somewhat different from life itself, and b) that works of art are experienced as whole structures of action, thought and feeling.

The most powerful forms of literary determinism in the twentieth century have derived from the work of Marx and Freud rather than that of Taine. The reason for this is clear.

The Tainean axiom that literature reflects culture and epoch leaves us at sea in a turbulent ocean of social and cultural themes with no guiding principles to find our way to land. Anything may be important, since the concept of reflection is far too vague to provide a clear interpretive principle. The traditions of Marx and Freud, on the other hand, set forth a clear conception of what themes are significant and a sophisticated method for relating these themes to each other and to the culture which produces them. In both cases, this method is essentially based on a concept of function; instead of the vagueness of the notion of reflection, we have in Marxian and Freudian criticism a commitment to the idea that literature can best be understood and analyzed through the way in which it accomplishes certain social or psychological functions. By focusing the interpretation around the concept of function, Marxian and Freudian criticism have the advantage of providing a uniform principle for the discussion of themes in relation to a conception of the whole work and of its social or psychological context.

While a full exposition of something as complex as Marxian or Freudian criticism is impossible in this essay, we can indicate in a generalized way the conceptions of function which these critical theories assume. From the Marxian point of view, the function of literature and the other arts is to express the ideology or fulfill some need of the social group or class which sponsors, produces or otherwise controls the work. As Marxian criticism has developed, the concept of ideology has been elaborated in increasingly sophisticated ways. Thus, while it is fairly easy to reject the primitive Marxian criticism which sees practically everything in modern European and American literature as a bourgeois plot against the working class—as in the pedantic Marxist criticism of the 1930s which reduced great writers like Henry James to object-lessons of bourgeois decadence and applauded the self-conscious proletarianism of such now-forgotten novels as Clara Weatherwax's *Marching, Marching*—we cannot so easily throw out the works of critics like George Lukacs and Raymond Williams. Indeed, the power of the Marxian approach to literary interpretation is such that it has been adopted in part by many critics and historians who are unsympathetic to the revolutionary aspects of Marxian politics. For example, in his essay "Ten-gallon Hero," David Brion Davis employs a method of analysis related to the Marxian tradition. In essence his approach to the Western is to interpret it as a reflection of the ideologies of regional and age groups in the United States. He argues, for instance, that certain elements of the Western represent the ideology of the pre-Civil War South "purified and regenerated by the casting off of apologies for slavery." Without the burden of defending slavery, the Southern ideology could "focus all energies on its former role of opposing the peculiar social and economic philosophy of the Northeast .... Asserting the importance of values beyond the utilitarian and material, this transplanted Southern philosophy challenged the doctrine of enlightened self-interest and the belief that leisure time is sin." Davis further argues that the Western expressed ideological traits of the American pre-adolescent:

The volume of cowboy magazines, radio programs and motion pictures, would indicate a national hero for at least a certain age group, a national hero who could hardly help but reflect specific attitudes. The cowboy myth has been chosen by this audience because it combines a complex of traits, a way of life, which they consider the proper ideal for America.[3]

In other words, the ideological approach to a work like the Western requires the definition and interpretation of narrative elements in relation to the social position of the work's primary audience. Thus, according to Davis, American pre-adolescents need to express their feelings of tension about the increasing responsibilities society is thrusting upon them. The cowboy hero provides them with an embodiment and justification of the "carefree life" of childhood and thereby expresses their social ideology.

Davis is not always clear about his conception of function. Another comment in his essay suggests a very different principle of explanation from the concept of ideological expression which he uses at other points.

Physical prowess is the most important thing for the ten-or-twelve-year-old mind. They are constantly plagued by fear, doubt, and insecurity, in short, by evil, and they lack the power to crush it. The cowboy provides the instrument for their aggressive impulses, while the villain symbolizes all evil.[4]

The last sentence of this quotation actually implies two different conceptions of function. To say that "the villain symbolizes all evil," though somewhat ambiguous, is conceivably consistent with the idea of ideological expression, since the statement may mean that the villain represents the social types or forces which the audience ideology defines as bad. However, the assertion that the cowboy "provides the instrument for their aggressive impulses" can only make sense as the expression of a psychological function. In this case, Davis implies that the pre-adolescent audience has feelings of hostility which need to be discharged in some fashion. Through a process of identification with the cowboy hero, the pre-adolescent audience performs aggressive acts against the villain and thereby relieves its own pent-up feelings. According to this line of interpretation, the elements of the Western (i.e. the clash between cowboy hero and villain) are determined by the capacity of these elements to perform a certain psychological function (i.e. to release the feelings of hostility and aggression). This kind of interpretation does not necessarily contradict the conception of ideological analysis. For example, the objects of aggression may be determined ideologically, at least in part. One of the favorite Western villains, the tyrannical and unscrupulous banker, could be interpreted as an ideological enemy of the pre-adolescent audience, since the banker represents the adult world of power, responsibility and respectability which the pre-adolescent seeks to reject. Similarly, it is quite possible to see certain psychological needs as determined by social position. One might argue that the high level of pre-adolescent aggressiveness is a result of the particular tensions which modern societies place on this age-group. It is quite possible, therefore, to create a kind of synthesis of Marxian and Freudian methods of explanation, and many contemporary critics have done so.

To clarify the situation a bit more, let us examine the conception of psychological function for a moment in isolation from the problem of social ideology. For ages, critics of literature have assumed some psychological basis for the appeal of the arts. Aristotle, for example, suggests that men enjoy literature because they find pleasure and instruction in the act of imitation. However, it was not until Freud fully developed his conception of manifold psychic processes operating beyond the full knowledge or control of the individual that psychological determinism became an important mode of literary analysis. Insofar as earlier theorists dealt with the problem of artistic determinants, it was usually in connection with some ideal of beauty or truth to which the artist might aspire by a combination of conscious choice and innate skill or genius. Freud's view that artistic form might be determined entirely or in part by psychological needs of which the artist and audience were not consciously aware gave plausibility and meaning for the first time to a view of art that would have seemed entirely paradoxical to most earlier thinkers: that art, which would seem by definition to be a matter of the most refined conscious choice, might be in fact the result of unconscious impulse. Since Freud, many critics have been interested in the psychological determinants of art, and in recent years some biologists such as Shepherd, Morris and Lorenz have even begun to form hypotheses about the related problem of the biological determinants of art. Two conceptions have dominated the discussion of psychological function: a) the idea that art appeals to people by vicariously satisfying deeply felt impulses or desires which cannot normally be fufilled, i.e. the conception of wish fulfillment; and b) the idea that art derives from some persistently disturbing psychic conflict which, failing of resolution in life, seeks it in the symbolic form of fantasy, i.e. the idea of repetition compulsion.

The passage from Davis' essay which I quoted above embodies a rather simplified form of the wish-fulfillment idea of function. The audience identifies with the hero, who performs violent actions, thereby gratifying the audience's own aggressive wishes, conscious or unconscious. A similar view connects popular literature with the wish-fulfillment of sexual impulses, as in the argument that James Bond is so appealing because he enables his readers to satisfy vicariously the sexual wishes that they cannot carry out in real life. Some critics held a sexual view of literature even before Freud. For example, many eighteenth and early nineteenth century moralists were convinced that novel-reading pandered to sinful impulses. Freud transformed the moralistic conception of wish-fulfillment by suggesting that the significant thing about the impulses which found expression in literary form was not their sinfulness but their unconscious character. In Freudian terms literature, like dreams, had to be at least partly understood as a disguised expression of wishes which the conscious mind was not prepared to admit. However, Freud's own conception of the psychological determinants of literature moved from the more simple conception of impulse gratification to the far more complex idea of repetition compulsion. According to Freud, many human impulses are not only blocked by the environment but are censored by the conscious mind because they represent desires too disturbing for the ego to consciously accept. However, these impulses continue to seek expression and fulfillment. Thus, a constant tension arises in the mind and ultimately these unconscious impulses find expression, sometimes in dreams, sometimes in neurotic behavior and sometimes in art.

The conception of repetition compulsion assumes that certain unresolved impulses—particularly those growing out of the relations between parents and children in the course of the child's psychological development—are so imperative that if he fails to resolve them in childhood, an individual is doomed to constantly re-experience these impulses and the psychic conflict they generate through various analogies and disguises. For example, a man who never satisfactorily resolves his sexual feelings about his mother, will, according to Freud, invariably find himself re-enacting the original sexual conflict in most of his future dealings with the opposite sex. In addition, this conflict is likely to shape the kind of art he creates and enjoys. An excellent example of this kind of analysis can be found in an essay by Dr. Kenneth J. Munden, "A Contribution to the Psychological Understanding of the Cowboy and his Myth."[5] Beginning with an analysis of the neurotic conflict of feelings in a cowboy patient, Dr. Munden seeks to show how this same conflict shapes the central themes of the Western.

The idea of repetition compulsion seems particularly

germane to the analysis of literary types like the Western or the detective story where certain character types and patterns of action are repeated in many different works. Indeed, it is tempting to hypothesize that strongly conventionalized narrative types like adventure and mystery stories, situation comedies and sentimental romances are so widely appealing because they enable people to re-enact and temporarily resolve widely shared psychic conflicts. Furthermore, this is an idea which can bring together social and psychological conceptions of function, since it is quite likely that the child-rearing practices and ideologies of different social groups have created characteristic psychic conflicts in various social groups or subcultures. These differences, in turn, might help account for changing themes and conventions in popular genres like the Western. Similarly, the characteristic psychological syndromes of different groups and periods may be partly responsible for the evolution of a variety of popular story types like the classical detective story, the hard-boiled detective story, the sentimental romance and the spy story.

If the function of resolving basic psychological tensions determines the structure of popular narrative types, we should be able to do two things. First, we must show that different story types are popular with particular social groups having characteristic psychic tensions; and second, we must delineate recurrent symbols and patterns in the narrative which generate and resolve these tensions. To some extent, this can be done. For example, the contrast between classical detective stories and pulp Western novels, such as those written by Max Brand, Ernest Haycox, Frank Gruber and Luke Short, does embody differences in audience, symbols and narrative pattern. The classical detective stories are more popular with urban, middle and upper-middle class readers of higher educational attainments and some intellectual bent. While it is not certain just what the proportion of men to women readers are for this type, it is clear that women are a very important audience element, perhaps even a dominant one—for no other type of literature has had so high a proportion of women among its most eminent practitioners: for example, Agatha Christie, Dorothy L. Sayers, Ngaio Marsh, Margery Allingham, Josephine Tey. The pulp Western, on the other hand, seems to be predominantly a masculine form, and its primary audience is the young and less highly educated. The Western is more popular with lower middle class readers from outside the major metropolitan areas. For example, in the city of Chicago, Westerns are less popular in the downtown areas than they are in the outlying city of Gary with its working-class population many of whom are recent migrants from rural areas of the South.

It is not too difficult to find a number of suggestive differences between the primary themes and symbols of these two story types and certain socio-psychological differences in these audience groups, which tend to support the functional idea of symbolic tension resolution. For example, the classical detective story is structured around the rationalistic uncovering of hidden guilt. The narrative movement in this kind of story is from a mysterious guilt which might prove to be the responsibility of anyone to a specific crime solved by the detective which is usually the action of some marginal person. The sense of guilt is one of the primary psychological mechanisms by which achievement-oriented members of the middle class have traditionally raised their children, which is why the psychological histories of successful people are so frequently shot through with the unbearable tensions caused by a guilty sense that they have not lived up to parental expectations. We might expect a narrative form in which a strong, authoritative detective demonstrates that someone else is guilty of a specific crime to provide a sense of temporary release for such people. Moreover, this line of reasoning provides a plausible explanation for the form's special popularity with upper middle-class women. Though similarly imbued by their upbringing with a strong achievement motive connected to a sense of guilt, upper middle-class women have traditionally been blocked from full participation in the masculine world of achievement. Therefore they are likely to feel a very strong tension between their inner drive for achievement and the actual level of accomplishments permitted by society. Such a tension could lead to an interest in stories in which an authoritative figure proves that someone else is guilty. Not surprisingly, the upper middle-class housewife is often a compulsive reader of detective stories.

The Western has a more various thematic content than the classical detective story; consequently it is more difficult to make simple generalizations about it. However, one major focus of the Western, particularly the pulp Western, is on the justification of acts of violent aggression. In other words, one of the major organizing principles of the Western is to so characterize the villains that the hero is both intellectually and emotionally justified in destroying them. Thus, it can be argued that the Western's narrative pattern works out and resolves the tension between a strong need for aggression and a sense of ambiguity and guilt about violence. As Dr. Munden indicates in his essay on the psychological dynamics of the Western, this kind of psychic tension is a classic symptom of the oedipus conflict. We would expect to find the compulsion to encounter and seek a resolution for this tension to be strongest among male adolescents. But, in addition, there are social-psychological reasons why this kind of tension also exists among lower middle and working class males, for in modern industrial societies, these groups are constantly subjected to the pressures of social change in such a way that their sense of masculine independence is continuously threatened. For blue-collar and white-collar workers at the lower echelons of the large industrial organization, or for independent farmers facing the increasing competition of large industrial organizations, the corporation plays somewhat the same psychological role as the father does for the adolescent boy: it is recognized as an inescapable authority upon whose benevolence the individual is dependent, yet at the same time, it is an object of the most violent hostility and a basic threat to the individual's ego. Couple this with the fact that the culture of working-class groups has traditionally placed a strong emphasis on masculine dominance, and it is not hard to see how the Western might fill an important psychological function for these groups.

These are only examples of the kinds of interpretation that can be constructed with the concept of social or psychological functions. Much more detailed and complex analyses can be made as the reader can see by consulting Dr. Munden's psychoanalytic study of the Western. Personally, I have no doubt that the concept of function is an important one for the study of popular literature. However, there are several major difficulties which must be overcome before we can begin to talk about the social or psychological functions of works of art with any assurance.

First, as commonly practiced, functional analysis tends to reduce the work of art to its performance of a single function. Thus, the psychonalytic critic sees the Western as an example of a repetition compulsion recapitulating a certain kind of oedipal conflict; the social critic sees the Western as an expression of the ideology of a certain group, etc. But unless these various functional explanations are mutually exclusive and only one can be right, we must accept the idea that a literary work has a variety of functions. Unfortunately, there seems to be little ground to argue for the exclusive validity of any of the various theories of functional analysis that have been set forth. Each one has rather persuasive arguments to set forth in favor of its own theoretical framework and each has been able to make a plausible analysis of the major structural elements of the Western in its own terms. Moreover, since our own experience suggests that most complex human actions have a variety of motives, there seems little reason not to assume that complex creations like works of art have a variety of functions. What, then, can give some structure to the functional analysis of art? What prevents us from saying that any critic who is imaginative enough to think up a conceivable social or psychological function for a work of art is not perfectly correct?

One possible solution to this problem is the conception of levels of function which is, in fact, built into both Freudian and Marxian systems. According to this conception, there is one kind of basic function which is the ultimate determinant of all human behavior, including artistic creation. Other kinds of function that can be discerned are in some sense derivative or secondary. For Freud, this basic dynamic is the process of human sexual development; for Marx, it is the economic evolution of society and the conflict of classes which this evolution gives rise to. If we accept this conception of a single basic dynamic, statements about other functions can be validated or rejected by their consistency or inconsistency with the underlying dynamic, for these other functions must be considered disguises or transformations of the basic function. However, though the concept of levels of function is more complex and interesting, and allows room for additional conceptions of function within the system, it is open to the same objections noted above: in the long run, it still reduces a variety of functions to a single basic dynamic. Moreover, in the interpretation of works of art which have so many possible meanings, there is an inevitable circularity in the Freudian or Marxian approach. It is a notorious truism that one can find almost anything one wants to in a work of art. If we begin our analysis with a conception of what is more important derived from external theoretical considerations, our interpretation will invariably validate the conception, since we will surely find the evidence we need. Can one imagine a work of art without some kind of conflict? Probably not. If it is a premise of our theory that the oedipal conflict is a universal human affliction, we will certainly find it in any work of art we look at. What then will we have discovered? Only that we have so defined oedipal conflict that it is synonymous with works of art.

Dr. Munden's approach to the Western is far more subtle and persuasive than this for two reasons. First of all, he uses clinical observation as a check against his literary interpretations. Thus, the principle of validation upon which psychoanalytic inquiry rests—the observation of the patient's response to the events of the consultation—can be at least partially applied to the interpretation of symbolic patterns in the work. Second, Dr. Munden seeks to isolate a particular form of the oedipal conflict which is characteristic of the Western and not of all literary works. However, even when carried out with Dr. Munden's sophistication, this kind of functional analysis still makes two problematic assumptions: a) that the creation and enjoyment of literary works are primarily activities with a single dominant psychological purpose; and b) that this purpose is predominantly one of achieving latent or unconscious goals. On the point of the first assumption, there is no particular reason to believe that the power of works of art can be best understood in terms of a single dominant psychological purpose. In fact, aestheticians since Aristotle have as often as not stressed a number of irreducible values—

such as pleasure and instruction—which works of art accomplish and for which they are treasured. If it is the case that works of art are used by human beings because they function in several different ways which cannot be synthesized or derived from a single basic cause, then a strictly psychological or social analysis of function can only result in a distorted interpretation, for it does not take into consideration all the relevant factors.

Such reflections not only cast doubt on those interpretations which depend on the conception of a single basic function, they also suggest that the very contrary may be the case—that the way to understand works of art, in functional terms, is to investigate the way in which they accomplish a maximal number of social and psychological functions. One might hypothesize then that a popular form like the Western comes into existence, not because it embodies a single basic psychological dynamic but because it fulfills more different social and psychological functions for its particular culture than other possible kinds of story. This hypothesis suggests an alternative principle for ordering our functional interpretation of literary works. Instead of seeing how the work expresses a basic psychological dynamic, this approach would lead us to ask how the artistic structure makes possible the unified accomplishment of the largest variety of social and psychological functions relevant to the cultural context.

Such a conception would also have to include— presumably under the rubric of psychological functions—some conception of the work of art's power to achieve goals of artistic pleasure or entertainment. This brings us to the second questionable assumption which I noted above: that the primary psychological function of works of art is the accomplishment of latent or unconscious goals. F.E. Emery in his essay "Psychological Effects of the Western Film" takes up this question and shows just how complex it is. For example, Emery questions whether the viewing of a Western can best be understood as subconscious goal-directed activity in the way which the psychoanalytic theory of psychological function assumes. He concludes that this approach is dubious both in the light of ordinary experience and experimental results:

The notion of a step-by-step movement towards a goal with

subsequent release of unwanted or painful tension on achieving it seems much more dubious as an explanation of [Western] viewing. To explain the course of viewing in this way one would have to equate the end of the story with the goal; otherwise one would be left with an unexplained period of viewing after the goals had been achieved. However, experience suggests that the end is not normally experienced as a release from unwanted tension; the end may in fact be accompanied by a sense of regret that it is all over, and in general is experienced as a more or less satisfying 'winding up' of the story (rather like a brandy after a heavy meal). That the end-as-such has little intrinsic psychological value is demonstrated by audience behavior when the 'winding-up' precedes or is obvious before the formal end—they begin to drift out of the situation or get restless.[6]

Emery goes on to suggest that "there is an alternative answer to the problem of what goes on in the viewing situation. This answer places the emphasis on the ... phenomena of enjoyment."[7] Unfortunately, Emery is not able to define just what "enjoyment" means with any fullness, but he does have two very suggestive insights. One arises from his very interesting treatment of the problem of identification. The reader will recall that the classical notion of art as "wish-fulfillment" assumes a direct identification between the hero and the audience; thus, when hero hits villain, the audience feels an immediate satisfaction of its aggressive impulses. However, as Emery points out, identification is not that simple a phenomenon. Though some kind of identification undoubtedly takes place, there are at least two factors that prevent this identification from becoming total: a) the viewer or reader is still conscious of the differences between himself and the hero; his own personal qualities, interests and values will make his identification a selective one; and b) the viewer always maintains a certain detachment or aesthetic distance from the action since he knows it is a work of art, or as Emery puts it, "the viewing situation exists at a *level of irreality* from the individual; it will be distinguished by him from real life in much the same way as he distinguishes dreams and play."[8]

The implications of this conception of selective and detached identification are very significant, and require some further reflection. First of all, we probably need to make a distinction between the level of detachment that obtains in a work like *Crime and Punishment* and a detective novel by

Mickey Spillane, or in a complex Western novel like Walter Van Tilburg Clark's *The Ox-Bow Incident* and a rootin'-tootin' shoot-'em up Western like one of the Hopalong Cassidy movies. In the two examples of serious novels, complex moral ambiguities, the absence of a clearly good and heroic protagonist, and the very quality of the style probably promote a greater level of aesthetic detachment. In the Spillane novel or the Cassidy film, everything works toward a more complete and total identification with the hero: the villains are clearly evil, the hero is morally pure, and the style invites our fullest and most unwitting participation in the hero's triumph over difficulties. Thus, we find that the audience for this type of art tends to make the greatest confusion between art and reality. This is probably the kind of identification which leads fans of soap operas to send presents to their favorite heroines and to weep unreservedly at the death of some beloved character. However, one can easily make too much of such phenomena. I think we would say that the number of persons who really confuse soap or horse opera with reality is very small. Instead, it is more likely that characters in popular programs on radio, TV or in films become precious to viewers not because they come to see them as real but because they become associated with a reliable kind of feeling which, whether happy or vaguely melancholy, is fundamentally an aesthetic one. Further evidence against the idea of total identification comes from the observation of children who one would think are most likely to confuse art with reality. In fact, as Sheldon Sacks points out in an essay on the psychological basis of genres, children reveal not only the ability to tell art from reality but the capacity to recognize the appropriate responses to different genres at a very early age:

Imagine a child watching respectively an animated cartoon in which a favorite, mischievous animal character is squashed into a pretty pancake-shaped object and the same child viewing a television episode of *Lassie* in which the noble collie is temporarily separated from her unhappy master. The first elicits laughter. The second tears, or, more moderately, anxiety, though surely in some everyday sense the mischievous cartoon figure is more seriously threatened than the noble dog. It is clear that in each case the child has made a correct intuitive judgment based on the manner in which the plight of a character is represented. In other words, he has had to intuit an artistic end to which such characters are represented from the manner in which they are represented.[9]

Another observation suggesting a similar conclusion comes from the Himmelweit study of the effects of television on children. Himmelweit observed that children were made far more anxious and fearful by the actions of serious adult drama than they were by the violence in Westerns. The reason, obviously, was that children had learned the pattern of artistic expectation and response appropriate to Westerns but had not come to understand some of the implications of more adult dramas. In sum, though popular entertainment literature probably evokes a more total identification between audience and hero, this is a relative matter. A strong degree of artistic detachment remains for all but the most confused and disturbed members of the audience.

Emery's conception of "enjoyment" derives from this idea of identification as reflecting the distinction between art and reality. Because the viewer defines the work of art as different from the real world, he will find himself able in the course of the artistic experience to relax the barriers that he has erected to protect his ego in the real world. Therefore he can come into more direct contact with the pattern of his inner needs:

This formulation, if true, leads to the important psychological consequence that what takes place in the film will, via the self-cum-hero, directly communicate with the more central regions of the personality (his primary concerns and needs), and not be mediated by the peripheral mundane pursuits and habits of thought and action that normally stand between a person and the outside world and between awareness of one's immediate concerns and of one's deeper self.[10]

Thus, for Emery, "enjoyment" comes from some kind of connection between the pattern or structure of elements in a work of art and a pattern of inner needs and tensions:

Individuals do not normally prefer a given theme because they see it as serving or satisfying some particular needs or sets of needs but because in viewing such a theme they experience some sense of 'fit' or harmony between it and certain of their own *unconscious* inner needs and tensions.[11]

This statement, vague as it is, seems more satisfactory than the simple functional determinism which postulates a direct causal relationship between a particular psychic tension and the elements of a work of art. First, this way of dealing with the relation between artistic elements and psychological needs as a matter of 'fit' or harmony enables us to consider the possibility that the work brings several different kinds of psychological and social functions into some kind of pattern related to the complex pattern of needs, interests and values in the audience. Second, and perhaps most important, this formulation enables us to consider the work of art not as a derivative of some social or psychological function but as an autonomous structure which arises from the possibilities of a unique kind of human experience: the representation or imitation of actions and things in such a way that the audience can feel strongly about them and yet remain detached. The next problem is to determine how we can arrive at an artistic definition of the Western and then return in a more complex way to the question of its socio-psychological significance.

II

An essay on the Western by Peter Homans[12] suggests a way of resolving some of these difficulties, though, in the end, it too falls into the trap of reducing an artistic construction to a simplistic cultural explanation. Mr. Homans approaches the Western by attempting to understand it as a unified construction before he tries to determine its cultural significance. His method, therefore, involves three main steps: 1) isolation of the characteristic elements—setting, characters, events, themes—of the Western; 2) analysis of the characteristic way in which the Western organizes these elements into an ordered pattern or plot; 3) determination of the cultural significance of this pattern.

Using this approach, Mr. Homans concludes that the basic pattern of the Western is a plot "in which evil appears as a series of temptations to be resisted by the hero—most of which he succeeds in avoiding through inner control. When faced with the embodiments of these temptations, his mode of control changes, and he destroys the threat. But the story is so structured that the responsibility for this act falls upon the adversary, permitting the hero to destroy while appearing to save."[13] This pattern, Mr. Homans feels, is related to the cultural influence of "Puritanism" because it has the same emphasis on the necessity for inner control and repression of "the spontaneous, vital aspects of life." The popularity of the Western, therefore, is to be attributed to its permitting a legitimated indulgence in violence while reasserting at the same time the "Puritan" norm of the primacy of will over feeling. Therefore, Mr. Homans believes there is a connection between the popularity of the Western and the cyclic outbursts of religious revivalism in the United States.

Despite some dubious historical generalizations, it seems to me that Mr. Homans' basic approach is unexceptional. He recognizes that the Western is not simply a collection of characters or themes, but an artistic construction which results in "an ordered vision of character, event and detail."[14] Furthermore, Homans points out that the analyst must not only identify typical settings, characters and events, but discover and state their relationship to each other in terms of some "basic organizing and interpretive principle for the myth as a whole."[15] The analyst must, in other words, define the action or plot in Aristotle's sense of the term. A statement of what happens, or a list of characters will not suffice, for events and characters in any dramatic work cannot be correctly interpreted except in relation to the structure of the whole work. Many critics point with alarm to the events of violence which occur so frequently in contemporary popular cultural forms, but simply to count with horrified fascination the number of beatings, murders, eye-gougings, etc., which one can encounter in a day of television viewing will lead to little in the way of illumination. Imagine what a viewer-with-alarm might say about a television program which began with a murder and moved through suicides, poisonings and suggestions of incest to end up with the screen littered with corpses. Pretty terrible, and doubtless indicative of the alienation, sadism and nihilism which dominates contemporary popular culture, except that these events were not taken from a television Western but from

Shakespeare's *Hamlet*. The point, of course, is that in an artistic construction, events, even violent ones, take their meaning from the whole structure. There is quantitatively just as much violence in Shakespeare or in *Oedipus the King* (a nice bit of eye-gouging) as there is in *Gunsmoke*, but it does not mean the same thing. In the Western violence is characteristically the hero's means of resolving the conflict generated by his adversary; in Shakespeare it is the means by which the hero destroys himself or is destroyed; in the classic detective story, violence is the adversary's means of protection and the hero's clue. In each instance violence cannot be understood simply as violence, for its meaning depends on the place it plays in the overall structure of the action.

Thus, the first step in the cultural analysis of any artistic construction must be the definition of its elements and their relations. In the case of a narrative or dramatic construction like the Western, the elements are characters, events, settings, themes or ideas and language, and the pattern is that of a plot or action in the sense of a unified chain of events growing out of the motives and ideas of a group of characters and having a definable beginning, middle and end.

Social scientists may well object at this point that the method of analysis I propose is essentially a humanistic approach and is therefore hopelessly subjective and unscientific, for everyone knows that humanists are continually quarreling over the interpretation of the works of art with which they deal. It is true that to isolate and quantify the elements of a pattern is apparently a more scientific procedure than the attempt to define their complex relationships to one another. But, as I have suggested, such a procedure is so false to the nature of artistic constructions that it is about as scientific as it would be to think one had analyzed an election by counting the number of polling places. Nor is the kind of plot analysis I have suggested as subjective as it seems, for there is the direct empirical test of whether the analyst's model of the plot actually fits the work itself, or, to put it another way, whether the suggested organizing principles actually account for the various elements in the work. A good plot model should provide a basis for explaining why each event and character is present in the work, and why these events and characters are placed in the setting they occupy. If some element remains unexplained, it is clear that the organizing principles have not been adequately stated.

III

Mr. Homans' careful discussion of a typical Western plot seems to me an excellent proof that such an analysis can be carried on carefully and objectively. Unfortunately in the case of Mr. Homans' analysis, a confusion between a typical Western plot and the Western as a popular form leads to a breakdown in his methodology and finally to an unwarrantedly simplistic conclusion. The reason for this is that there is an important difference from a methodological point of view between the Western and, say, a novel by Henry James. The latter is a unique construction shaped by a highly individual artist, while the former is a general type with many different particular versions. In studying the cultural significance of a work by Henry James we are dealing with the vision and creative power of a unique individual. In other words, a novel by James is, because of its uniqueness, a type in itself. However, in analyzing a popular form like the Western, we are *not* primarily concerned with an individual work, such as a single episode of *Gunsmoke* or a particular novel by Zane Grey, but with the cultural significance of the Western as a type of artistic construction. This is simply because the circumstances in which a Western is produced and consumed do not encourage the creation of unique individual works of art but lead to the production of particular realizations of a conventional formula. Therefore the culturally significant phenomenon is not the individual work but the formula or recipe by which more or less anonymous producers turn out individual novels or films. The individual works are ephemeral, but the formula lingers on, evolving and changing with time, yet still basically recognizable. Therefore, a popular form, like the Western, may encompass a number of standard plots. Indeed, one important reason for the continued use of a formula is its very ability to change and develop in response to the changing interests of audiences. A formula which cannot be adapted like this will tend to disappear. One good illustration of this is the immensely popular nineteenth century form of the moralistic, sentimental novel of seduction which grew out of Richardson's *Pamela*. In the twentieth century the cultural patterns which made this form of narrative meaningful and exciting have changed too much for the form to adapt to them. Other popular formulas, like the Western and the detective story, have thus far proved more adaptable to changing cultural needs.

The trouble with Homans' analysis is that he takes one typical plot for *the* Western. There are many Westerns of the type Homans describes in which an outsider comes into a community, is tempted by evil, overcomes the temptation, destroys the evil and leaves again. On the other hand, there are a good many Westerns in which the central action is the initiation of the hero into the world of men—as in stories of the dude-become-hero variety—in which the plot hinges on the resolution through violence of a conflict between love and social prejudice—as in Owen Wister's classic *The Virginian*. What we need is plot analyses comparable to those Homans has given us of the several standard Western plots. From such analyses we shall be able to discern more clearly than before the general outlines of the formula by discovering those patterns which run through all the types of Western plot. In addition, these plot models would certainly tell us a great deal about the changing significance of the Western, for I have no doubt that, if we were able to classify the types of Western plots, we would find that certain plots have been particularly popular at different times. Being able to trace changes within the formula should enable us to discover many important things about changes in the culture which produced it, and there is no better way of defining these changes than through a comparison of plots.

IV

But what is the formula of the Western, and how can we best define it? What is the most effective way of generalizing about the various plot models which have been associated with the Western during its long history?

The most important generalizing concept which has been

applied to cultural studies in recent years is that of myth. Indeed, it could be argued that the concept of formula which I am developing is simply another variation on the idea of myth. But if this is the case, I would argue that distinctions between meanings of the concept of myth are worth making and naming, for myth now has too many different meanings. Some people use the term myth in a way which hardly separates it from the concept of theme, as when we talk about the myth of progress or the myth of success. There is also another common meaning of the term which further obfuscates its use, namely myth as a common belief which is demonstrably false. Many cultural studies are organized around this opposition between myth and reality. Thus, when a critic uses the term myth one must first get clear whether he means to say that the object he is describing is a false belief or simply a belief, or something still more complicated like an archetypal pattern. Moreover, because of the special connection of the term myth with a group of stories which have survived from ancient cultures, particularly the Greco-Roman, the scholar who uses the concept in the analysis of contemporary popular culture sometimes finds himself drawn into another kind of reductionism which takes the form of attributing the impact of contemporary popular forms to their occasional plot parallels with classical myths.

Because of this great confusion about the term myth, I suggest we differentiate the concept of formula from that of myth, thereby giving us two more clearly defined generalizing concepts to work with.

In defining formula, let me begin with a kind of axiom or assumption which I hope I can persuade you to accept without elaborate argumentation: all cultural products contain a mixture of two elements: conventions and inventions. Conventions are elements which are known to both the creator and his audience beforehand—they consist of things like favorite plots, stereotyped characters, accepted ideas, commonly known metaphors and other linguistic devices, etc. Inventions, on the other hand, are elements which are uniquely imagined by the creator such as new kinds of characters, ideas or linguistic forms. Of course it is difficult to distinguish in every case between conventions and inventions because many elements lie somewhere along a continuum between the two poles. Nonetheless, familiarity with a group of literary works will usually soon reveal what the major conventions are and therefore what elements are unique to an individual work.

Convention and invention have quite different cultural functions. Conventions represent familiar shared images and meanings and they assert an ongoing continuity of values; inventions confront us with a new perception or meaning which we have not realized before. Both these functions are important to culture. Conventions help maintain a culture's stability while inventions help it respond to changing circumstances and provide new information about the world. The same thing is true on the individual level. If the individual does not encounter a large number of conventionalized experiences and situations the strain on his sense of continuity and identity will lead to great tensions and even to neurotic breakdowns. On the other hand, without new information about his world, the individual will be increasingly unable to cope with it and will withdraw behind a barrier of conventions as some people withdraw from life into a compulsive reading of detective stories.

Most works of art contain a mixture of convention and invention. Both Homer and Shakespeare show a large proportion of conventional elements mixed with inventions of great genius. *Hamlet*, for example, depends on a long tradition of stories of revenge, but only Shakespeare could have invented a character who embodies so many complex perceptions of life that every generation is able to find new ways of viewing him. So long as cultures were relatively stable over long periods of time and homogeneous in their structure, the relation between convention and invention in works of literature posed relatively few problems. Since the Renaissance, however, modern cultures have become increasingly heterogeneous and pluralistic in their structure and discontinuous in time. In consequence, while public communications have become increasingly conventional in order to be understood by broad and diverse audiences, the intellectual elites have placed ever higher valuation on invention out of a sense that rapid cultural changes require continually new perceptions of the world. Thus we have arrived at a situation in which the model great work of literature is Joyce's *Finnegans Wake*, a creation which is almost as far as possible along the continuum toward total invention as it is possible to go without leaving the possibility of shared meanings behind. At the same time, there has developed a vast amount of literature characterized by the highest degree of conventionalization.

This brings us to an initial definition of formula. A formula is a conventional system for structuring cultural products. It can be distinguished from invented structures which are new ways of organizing works of art. Like the distinction between convention and invention, the distinction between formula and structure can be best envisaged as a continuum between two poles; one pole is that of a completely conventional structure of conventions—an episode of the Long Ranger or one of the Tarzan books comes close to this pole; the other end of the continuum is a completely original structure which orders inventions—*Finnegans Wake* is perhaps the ultimate example of this, though one might also cite such examples as Resnais' film *Last Year at Marienbad*, T.S. Eliot's poem *The Waste Land* or Beckett's play *Waiting for Godot*. All of these works not only manifest a high degree of invention in their elements but unique organizing principles. *The Waste Land*, for example, contains a substantial number of conventional elements—even to the point of using quotations from past literary works—but these elements are restructured in such a fashion that a new perception of familiar elements is forced upon the reader.

I would like to emphasize that the distinction between invented structure and formula as I am using it here is a descriptive rather than a qualitative one. Though it is likely for a number of reasons that a work possessing more invention than formula will be a greater work, we should avoid this easy judgment in our study of popular culture. In distinguishing invented structures from formulas we are trying to deal with the relationship between the work and its culture, and not with its artistic quality. Whether or not a different set of aesthetic criteria are necessary in the judgment of invented as opposed to formulaic works is an important and interesting question, but necessarily the subject of another series of reflections.

We can further differentiate the conception of formula by

comparing it to genre and myth. Genre, in the sense of tragedy, comedy, romance, etc., seems to be based on a difference between basic attitudes or feelings about life. I find Northrop Frye's suggestion that the genres embody fundamental mythic patterns reflecting stages of the human life cycle a very fruitful idea here.[16] For Frye myths are universal patterns of action which manifest themselves in all human cultures. Following Frye, let me briefly suggest a formulation of this kind—genre can be defined as a structural pattern which embodies a universal life pattern or myth in the materials of language. Formula, on the other hand, is cultural; it represents the way in which a particular culture has embodied both mythical archetypes and its own preoccupations in narrative form. Sheldon Sacks suggests another interesting hypothesis about the nature of genres: that they are known intuitively by human beings because the human mind possesses innate capacities to make distinctions between the comic and the tragic. For our purposes, however, Sacks' view, if correct, is no different in its consequences than Frye's. Genre is universal, basic to human perceptions of life.

An example will help clarify this distinction. The Western and the spy story can both be seen as embodiments of the archetypal pattern of the hero's quest which Frye discusses under the general heading of the mythos of romance. Or if we prefer psychoanalytic archetypes, these formulas embody the oedipal myth in fairly explicit fashion, since they deal with the hero's conquest of a dangerous and powerful figure. However, though we can doubtless characterize both Western and spy stories in terms of these universal archetypes, we have not thereby explained the basic and important differences in setting, characters and action between the Western and the spy story. These differences are clearly cultural and they reflect the particular preoccupations and needs of the time in which they were created and the group which created them: the Western shows its nineteenth century American origin while the spy story reflects the fact that it is largely a twentieth century British creation. Of course a formula articulated by one culture can be taken over by another. However, we will often find important differences in the formula as it moves from one culture or from one period to another. For example, the gunfighter Western of the 1950s is importantly different from the cowboy romances of Owen Wister and Zane Grey, just as the American spy stories of Donald Hamilton differ from the British secret agent adventures of Eric Ambler and Graham Greene.

The cultural nature of formulas suggests two further points about them. First, while myths, because of their basic and universal nature turn up in many different manifestations, formulas, because of their connection to a particular culture and period of time, tend to have a much more limited repertory of plots, characters and settings. For example, the pattern of action known generally as the Oedipus myth can be discerned in an enormous range of stories from *Oedipus Rex* to the latest Western. Indeed, the very difficulty with the myth as an analytical tool is that it is so universal that it hardly serves to differentiate one story from another. Formulas, however, are much more specific: Westerns must have a certain kind of setting, a particular cast of characters, and follow a limited number of lines of actions. A Western that does not take place in the West, near the frontier, at a point in history when social order and anarchy are in tension, and that does not involve some form of pursuit, is simply not a Western. A detective story that does not involve the solution of a mysterious crime is not a detective story. This greater specificity of plot, character and setting reflects a more limited framework of interests, values and tensions that relate to culture rather than to the generic nature of man.

The second point is a hypothesis about why formulas come into existence and enjoy such wide popular use. Why of all the infinite possible subjects for fictions do a few like the adventures of the detective, the secret agent and the cowboy so dominate the field?

Reverting to an earlier point, I suggest that formulas are important because they provide a model for the construction of artistic works which synthesize several important cultural functions which, in modern cultures have been partly taken over by the popular arts. Let me suggest just one or two examples of what I mean. In earlier, more homogeneous cultures, religious ritual performed the important function of articulating and reaffirming the primary cultural values.

Today, with cultures composed of a multiplicity of differing religious groups, the synthesis of values and their reaffirmation has become an increasingly important function of the mass media and the popular arts. Thus, one important dimension of formula is social or cultural ritual. Homogeneous cultures also possessed a large repertory of games and songs which all members of the culture understood and could participate in both for a sense of group solidarity and for personal enjoyment and recreation. Today the great spectator sports provide one way in which a mass audience can participate in games together. Artistic formulas also fulfill this function in that they constitute entertainments with rules known to everyone. Thus, a very wide audience can follow a Western, appreciate its fine points and vicariously participate in its pattern of suspense and resolution.

The game dimension of formulas has two aspects. First, there is the patterned experience of excitement, suspense and release which we associate with the functions of entertainment and recreation. Second, there is the aspect of play as ego-enchantment through the temporary resolution of inescapable frustrations and tensions through fantasy. As Piaget sums up this aspect of play:

> Conflicts are foreign to play, or, if they do occur, it is so that the ego may be freed from them by compensation or liquidation whereas serious activity has to grapple with conflicts which are inescapable. The conflict between obedience and individual liberty is, for example, the affliction of childhood [and, we might note, a key theme of the Western] and in real life the only solutions to this conflict are submission, revolt, or cooperation which involves some measure of compromise. In play, however, the conflicts are transposed in such a way that the ego is revenged, either by suppression of the problem or by giving it an acceptable solution ... it is because the ego dominates the whole universe in play that it is freed from conflict.[17]

Thus the game dimension of formula is a culture's way of simultaneously entertaining itself and of creating an acceptable pattern of temporary escape from the serious restrictions and limitations of human life. In formula stories, the detective always solves the crime, the hero always determines and carries out true justice, and the agent accomplishes his mission or at least preserves himself from the omnipresent threats of his enemy.

Finally, formula stories seem to be one way in which the individuals in a culture act out certain unconscious or repressed needs, or express in an overt and symbolic fashion certain latent motives which they must give expression to, but cannot face openly. This is the most difficult aspect of formula to pin down. Many would argue that one cannot meaningfully discuss latent contents or unconscious motives beyond the individual level or outside of the clinical context. Certainly it is easy to generate a great deal of pseudo-psychoanalytic theorizing about literary formulas and to make deep symbolic interpretations which it is clearly impossible to substantitate convincingly. However, though it may be difficult to develop a reliable method of analysis of this aspect of formulas, I am convinced that the Freudian insight that recurrent myths and stories embody a kind of collective dreaming process is essentially correct and has an important application on the cultural as well as the universal level, that is, that the idea of a collective dream applies to formula as well as to myth. But there is no doubt that we need to put more thought into our approach to these additional dimensions of formula and about their relation to the basic dimension of a narrative construction.

My argument, then, is that formula stories like the detective story, the Western, the seduction novel, the biblical epic and many others are structures of narrative conventions which carry out a variety of cultural functions in a unified way. We can best define these formulas as principles for the selection of certain plots, characters and settings which possess in addition to their basic narrative structure the dimensions of collective ritual, game and dream. To analyze these formulas we must first define them as narrative structures of a certain kind and then investigate how the additional dimensions of ritual, game and dream have been synthesized into the particular patterns of plot, character and setting which have become associated with the formula. It is now time to apply this conception to the analysis of the Western. After a brief glance at the vast range of material which embodies the formula of the Western, we must turn our attention to a preliminary attempt to define the conventions of setting, character and situation which, when structured in a particular way, constitute the formula of the Western.

V

The Western was created in the early nineteenth century by James Fenimore Cooper. Cooper's initial invention of the Leatherstocking (*The Pioneers*, 1823) paved the way for many fictional treatments of the West which strongly resembled his patterns of plot, character and theme (e.g. R.M. Bird's *Nick of the Woods* and W.G. Simms' *The Yemassee*). By 1860 these patterns had become sufficiently stereotyped that they could serve Edward Ellis as the basis of his *Seth Jones; or The Captives of the Frontier*, one of the most successful early dime novels. In the later nineteenth century, the Western formula continued to flourish in the dime novel and in popular drama. Even the autobiographical narratives of Western experiences and popular biographies of western heroes like Kit Carson, Buffalo Bill and General Custer, increasingly reflected the main elements of the formula, which was finally enshrined in the great spectacle of the Wild West Show. Gradually the cowboy replaced the frontier scout as the archetypal Western hero. Finally, in a number of works published around the turn of the century, the most important of which was Owen Wister's bestseller *The Virginian*, the western formula arrived at most of the characteristics it has held through innumerable novels, stories, films and TV shows in the twentieth century.

In one sense the Western formula is far easier to define than that of the detective story, for when we see a couple of characters dressed in ten-gallon hats and riding horses we know we are in a Western. On the other hand, the Western formula contains a greater variety of plot patterns than the detective story with its single line of criminal investigation. Frank Gruber, a veteran writer of pulp Westerns, suggests that there are seven basic Western plots: 1) The Union Pacific Story centering around the construction of a railroad, telegraph or stagecoach line or around the adventures of a wagon train; 2) The Ranch Story with its focus on conflicts between ranchers and rustlers or cattlemen and sheepmen; 3) The Empire Story, which is an epic version of the Ranch Story; 4) The Revenge

Story; 5) Custer's Last Stand, or the Cavalry and Indian Story;
6) The Outlaw Story; and 7) The Marshal Story. One could
doubtless construct other lists of plots that have been used in
Westerns, though Gruber's seems quite adequate. Later, I will
suggest that there is a kind of action pattern that the Western
tends to follow whether it be about ranchers, cavalrymen,
outlaws or marshals, but the possibility of such diversity of
plot patterns suggests that we know a Western primarily by the
presence of ten-gallon hats and horses. In other words, the
Western formula is initially defined by its setting. Therefore in
analyzing the components of the Western formula I will deal
initially with the setting.

1)   Setting

Tentatively we might say that the Western setting is a
matter of geography and costume; that is, a Western is a story
that takes place somewhere in the western United States in
which the characters wear certain distinctive styles of
clothing. However, this formulation is clearly inadequate since
there are many stories set in the American West which we
would not call Westerns under any circumstances, for example
the novels and stories of Hamlin Garland or Ole Rolvaag.
Moreover, there are novels set in the eastern United States
which are really Westerns, for example, the Leatherstocking
Tales of James Fenimore Cooper. Our geographical definition
must immediately be qualified by a social and historical
definition of setting: the Western is a story which takes place
on or near a frontier and consequently the Western is generally
set at a particular moment in the past.

The portrayal of the frontier in the Western formula differs
significantly from Frederick Jackson Turner's frontier thesis.
For Turner, the frontier was less important as "the meeting
point between savagery and civilization" than as a social and
economic factor in American history. His well-known frontier
thesis consisted of two central propositions: first, because the
American frontier lay "at the hither edge of free land" it had
maintained the democratic mobility and fluidity of American
life; and second, there tended to grow up in frontier settlements

a distinctively individualistic way of life which continually
revitalized the democratic spirit in America. Though a view of
the frontier resembling Turner's sometimes plays a role in the
structure of more complex and serious Westerns, the central
purport of the frontier in most Westerns has simply been its
potential as a setting for exciting, epic conflicts. The Western
formula tends to portray the frontier as "meeting point
between civilization and savagery" because the clash of
civilization ("law and order") with savagery, whether
represented by Indians or lawless outlaws, generates dramatic
excitement and striking antitheses without raising basic
questions about American society or about life in general. In
the Western formula savagery is implicitly understood to be on
the way out. It made no difference whether the creator of the
Western viewed savagery as a diabolical or criminal force (as
in most of the dime novels) or as a meaningful way of life for
which he felt a certain degree of elegiac nostalgia (an attitude
in many Westerns from Cooper to the movies of John Ford),
there was never a question that savagery might prevail, just as
in the detective story there is never really a doubt that the
criminal will ultimately be caught. While one might seriously
seek to espouse certain "natural" values and to reject those of
society (e.g. as in Thoreau's *Walden* or Whitman's poetry) and
while an American character in a novel by Henry James might
be deeply torn between the European and American ways of
life, the Western hero never has to make a basic choice like this,
for, insofar as he is a hero it must be in relation to the victory of
civilization over savagery, even if this victory, as it often does,
puts him out of a job. Edwin Fussell suggests that in the first
half of the nineteenth century the frontier retained enough of
an air of mystery that it could represent a fundamental
confrontation between human history and the possibility of a
society transcending it. However, Fussell believes that as
actual settlement progressed, the frontier lost its power as a
fundamental moral antithesis to society. By 1850, according to
Fussell, the frontier had ceased to be a major theme for the
greatest American writers. Fussell's discussion supplements
Henry Nash Smith's definition of the mythical West as the
potential locus of a new and more natural human society. Like
Fussell, Smith defines the early American conception of the

frontier as a serious antithesis to existing society. However, Smith believes that the romanticization of nature implicit in this conception of the frontier could never support a serious literature. Thus, after Cooper, the Western story declined to a point where "devoid alike of ethical and social meaning, [it] could develop in no direction save that of a straining and exaggeration of its formulas."[18]

Smith's treatment of the Western story is a bit harsh, ignoring as it does the rich flourishing of the Western in literature and on film in the twentieth century. However, Smith is essentially correct in pointing out that the Western formula has been an artistic device for resolving problems rather than confronting their irreconcilable ambiguities. Therefore the frontier setting and the role of the savage have invariably been defined in the formula as occasions for action rather than as the focus of the analysis.

In other words, the Indian rarely stands for a possible alternative way of life which implies a serious criticism of American society. Instead he poses a problem for the hero. Leslie Fiedler points out how often the complex relationship between a young white boy and an Indian or Negro is the central theme of major American novels. In his recent study, *The Return of the Vanishing American,* Fiedler argues that the Indian way of life has become an important counter-cultural symbol for many young radicals. But the Indian never plays such a role in the formula Western, because he is always in the process of vanishing. In fact, the treatment of the Indian in the formula Western bears out Roy Harvey Pearce's analysis of the American idea of savagism. Pearce shows how the various seventeenth and eighteenth century views of the Indian with their complex dialectic between the Indian as devil and as noble savage quickly gave way in the nineteenth century to a definition of the Indian way of life as an inferior and earlier stage in the development of civilization. This redefinition of the Indian justified his assimilation or extermination and therefore served the need of nineteenth century American society for a philosophical rationale to justify its brutal elimination of the native Indian cultures. Even in Westerns quite sympathetic to the Indian, such as John Ford's version of Mari Sandoz' *Cheyenne Autumn,* the focus of the action usually shifts from the Indians themselves to the dilemmas their situation poses for the white hero and heroine. In short, the Western formula seems to prescribe that the Indian be a part of the setting to a greater extent than he is ever a character in his own right. The reason for this is twofold: to give the Indian a more complex role would increase the moral ambiguity of the story and thereby blur the sharp dramatic conflicts; and second, if the Indian represented a significant way of life rather than a declining savagery, it would be far more difficult to resolve the story with a reaffirmation of the values of modern society.[19]

Taken together, the works of Smith, Fussell and Pearce suggest that the Western formula emerged as American attitudes toward the frontier gradually underwent significant change around the middle of the nineteenth century. It was possible for Americans in the early nineteenth century to treat the frontier as a symbol of fundamental moral antitheses between man and nature, and, consequently, to use a frontier setting in fiction that engaged itself with a profound exploration of the nature and limitations of man and society. However, the redefinition of the frontier as a place where advancing civilization met a declining savagery changed the frontier setting into a locus of conflicts which were always qualified and contained by the knowledge that the advance of civilization would largely eliminate them. Or, to put it another way, the frontier setting now provided a fictional justification for enjoying violent conflicts and the expression of lawless force without feeling that they threatened the values or the fabric of society.

Thus, the social and historical aspects of setting are perhaps even more important in defining the Western formula than geography. The Western story is set at a certain moment in the development of American civilization, namely at that point when savagery and lawlessness are in decline before the advancing wave of law and order, but are still strong enough to pose a local and momentarily significant challenge. In the actual history of the West, this moment was probably a relatively brief one in any particular area. In any case, the complex clashes of different interest groups over the use of Western resources and the pattern of settlement surely involved more people in a more fundamental way than the struggle with Indians or outlaws. Nonetheless, it is the latter which has become central to the Western formula. The relatively brief stage in the social evolution of the West when outlaws or Indians posed a threat to the community's stability has been erected into a timeless epic past in which heroic individual defenders of law and order without the vast social resources of police and courts stand poised against the threat of lawlessness or savagery. But it is also the nature of this epic moment that the larger forces of civilized society are just waiting in the wings for their cue. However threatening he may appear at the moment, the Indian is vanishing and the outlaw about to be superseded. It is because they too represent this epic moment that we are likely to think of such novels as Cooper's *Last of the Mohicans*, Bird's *Nick of the Woods*, or more recent historical novels like Walter Edmonds' *Drums Along the Mohawk* as Westerns, though they are not set in what we have come to know as the West.

Why then has this epic moment been primarily associated in fiction with a particular West, that of the Great Plains and the mountains and deserts of the "Far West" and with a particular historical moment, that of the heyday of the open range cattle industry of the later nineteenth century? Westerns can be set at a later time—some of Zane Grey's stories take place in the twenties and some, like those of Gene Autry, Roy Rogers or "Sky King" in the present—but even at these later dates the costumes and the represented way of life tend to be those of the later nineteenth century. Several factors probably contributed to this particular fixation of the epic moment. Included among these would be the ideological tendency of Americans to see the Far West as the last stronghold of certain traditional values, as well as the peculiar attractiveness of the cowboy hero. But more important than these factors, the Western requires a means of isolating and intensifying the drama of the frontier encounter between social order and lawlessness. For this purpose, the geographic setting of the Great Plains and adjacent areas has proved particularly appropriate, especially since the advent of film and television have placed a primary emphasis on visual articulation. Four characteristics of the Great Plains topography have been especially important: its openness, its aridity and general inhospitality to human life, its great extremes of light and climate, and, paradoxically, its grandeur and beauty. These topographic features create an effective backdrop for the action of the Western because they exemplify in visual images the thematic conflict between civilization and savagery and its resolution. In particular, the Western has come to center about the image of the isolated town or ranch or fort surrounded by the vast open grandeur of prairie or desert and connected to the rest of the civilized world by a railroad, a stagecoach or simply a trail. This tenuous link can still be broken by the forces of lawlessness, but never permanently. We can conceive it as a possibility that the town will be swept back into the desert—the rickety wooden buildings with their tottering false fronts help express the tenuousness of the town's position against the surrounding prairie—nonetheless we do not see the town solely as an isolated fort in hostile country—like an outpost of the French foreign legion in *Beau Geste*—but as the advance guard of an oncoming civilization. Moreover, while the prairie or desert may be inhospitable, it is not hostile. Its openness, freshness and grandeur also play an important role in the Western. Thus, the open prairie around the town serves not only as a haven of lawlessness and savagery, but as a backdrop of epic magnitude and even, at times, as a source of regenerating power.

This characteristic setting reflects and helps dramatize the tripartite division of characters that dominates the Western pattern of action. The townspeople hover defensively in their settlement, threatened by the outlaws or Indians who are associated with the inhospitable and uncontrollable elements of the surrounding landscape. The townspeople are static and largely incapable of movement beyond their little settlement. The outlaws or savages can move freely across the landscape. The hero, though a friend of the townspeople, has the lawless power of movement in that he, like the savages, is a horseman and possesses skills of wilderness existence. The moral character of the hero also appears symbolically in the Western setting. In its rocky aridity and climatic extremes the Great Plains landscape embodies the hostile savagery of Indians and outlaws, while its vast openness, its vistas of snow-covered peaks in the distance, and its great sunrises and sunsets (in the purple prose of Zane Grey, for example) suggest the epic courage and regenerative power of the hero. Thus, in every respect, Western topography helps dramatize more intensely the clash of characters and the thematic conflicts of the story. These dramatic resources of setting can of course be used more or less skillfully by the Western writer or film director, but even at their flattest they have a tendency to elevate rather commonplace plots into epic spectacles. When employed with conscious and skillful intent, as in the Western films of John Ford, the lyrical and epic power of landscape can sometimes transcend even the inherent limitations of popular culture and raise escapist adventure to a level of high artistry.

The special qualities of the Western setting emerge still more clearly from a comparison with the treatment of setting in the colonial adventure novels of English writers like H. Rider Haggard. Since it too involved adventures on the periphery of what its readers defined as civilization, the colonial adventure is the closest European analogue to the American Western. Like the Western setting, the tropical jungles of the colonial adventure have both hostile and attractive qualities. Haggard's African veldts, like the Western plains, contain savagery and raw nature which threaten the representatives of civilization. They are also full of exotic animals, beautiful natural spectacles, glamorous and mysterious cults, hidden treasures and other exciting secrets. But, in contrast to the fresh and open grandeur of the Western landscape, these double qualities of the colonial jungle are superficially attractive, but essentially subversive and dangerous. They are associated not with a redeeming hero who saves civilization from the threat of lawlessness and savagery, but with temptations which undermine the hero's commitment to civilization. The Western landscape can become the setting for a regenerated social order once the threat of lawlessness has been overcome, but the colonial landscape remains alien. Its doubleness simply reflects the difference between the overt threat of savage hostility and the more insidious danger of the attractiveness of alien cults and exotic ways of life. Perhaps because it contains an unresolved antithesis between man and jungle, the colonial adventure has inspired truly profound works of literature, as instanced by such examples as Joseph Conrad's *Heart of Darkness*, while the Western formula has at best produced good novels like Wister's *The Virginian* or Clark's *The Ox-Bow Incident.*

The first major writer who brought together the tripartite division of townsmen, savages and intermediate hero with a vision of the landscape was James Fenimore Cooper, who thereby became the creator of the Western. Even though Cooper's novels are set in the Eastern forests and many of his thematic emphases are quite different from the later Western, his landscapes show the same basic pattern. The new settlement (*The Pioneers*) or fort (*The Last of the Mohicans, The Pathfinder*) or "ranch" (Hutter's "castle" in *The Deerslayer*) is surrounded by miles of forested wilderness. It is clear, however, that civilization has irreversibly begun its advance. Like many later Western writers, Cooper liked frequently to call his reader's attention to the difference between the peaceful settlements of "today" and the dark mysterious forests of the earlier period of the story, thus insuring that the reader knew he was dealing with a stage of historical development which was definitely in the past. It is implicit in such a setting that the conflict between settlement and wilderness will soon be resolved. Cooper's wilderness also exemplifies the doubleness of the Western formula landscape. The forest is dark and frightening, but also the place where one gets the strongest feeling of the divine presence; it is the locus of the bloodthirsty and savage "Mingos" but also of the noble and heroic Delawares.

I have now discussed the effectiveness of the Western setting as both background and source of dramatic conflicts and have indicated its potentiality both as a means of exploring certain historical themes and as a way of evoking a sense of epic grandeur. But we must not forget that one reason for the success of the Western as a popular form in the twentieth century has been its unique adaptability to film. Two major characteristics of the Western setting turned out to have an enormous potential for cinematic expression: its great openness of space and its powerful visual contrasts.

The special openness of the topography of the Great Plains and western desert has made it particularly expressive for the portrayal of movement. Against the background of this terrain, a skillful director can create infinite variations of space ranging from long panoramas to close-ups and he can clearly articulate movement across these various spaces. No matter how often one sees it, there is something inescapably effective about that scene, beloved of Western directors, in which a rider appears like an infinitely small dot at the far end of a great empty horizon and then rides toward us across the intervening space, just as there is a different thrill about the vision of a group of horses and men plunging pell-mell from the foreground into the empty distance. Nor is there anything which quite matches the feeling of suspense when the camera picks up a little group of wagons threading their way across the middle distance and then pans across the arid rocks and up the slopes of a canyon until it suddenly comes upon a group of Indians waiting in ambush. Moreover, the western landscape is uniquely adaptable to certain kinds of strong visual effects because of the sharp contrasts of light and shadow characteristic of an arid climate together with the topographical contrasts of plain and mountain, rocky outcrops and flat deserts, steep bare canyons and forested plateaus. The characteristic openness and aridity of the topography also makes the contrast between man and nature and between wilderness and society visually strong.

Perhaps no film exploits the visual resources of the Western landscape more brilliantly than John Ford's 1939 *Stagecoach*. After a brief introduction the film opens on a street in one of those western shanty towns characterized by rickety false fronts. By the rushing motion of horses and wagons along the street and by the long vista down the street and out into the desert we are immediately made aware of the surrounding wilderness and of the central theme of movement across it which will dominate the film. This opening introduction of the visual theme of fragile town contrasted with epic wilderness will be developed throughout the film in the contrast between the flimsy stagecoach and the magnificent landscape through which it moves. Similarly, the restless motion of the opening scene will be projected into the thrust of the stagecoach across the landscape. This opening is followed by several brief scenes leading up to the departure of the stagecoach. These scenes are cut at a rather breathless pace so that they do not slow down the sense of motion and flight generated by the opening. Visually, they dwell on two aspects of the town, its dark, narrow and crowded interiors and its ramshackle sidewalks and storefronts, thus establishing in visual terms the restrictive and artificial character of town life. Then the stagecoach departs on its voyage and we are plunged into the vast openness and grandeur of the wilderness with the crowded wooden stagecoach serving as a visual reminder of the narrow town life it has left behind. Ford chose to shoot the major portion of the stagecoach's journey in Monument Valley, a brilliant choice because the visual characteristics of that topography perfectly embody the complex mixture of epic grandeur and savage bestiality that the film requires. The valley itself is a large, flat desert between steep hills. Thrusting up out of the valley floor gigantic monoliths of bare rock dwarf the stagecoach as it winds across this vast panorama. This combination of large open desert broken by majestic upthrusts of rock and surrounded by threatening hills creates an enormously effective visual environment for the story, which centers around the way in which the artificial social roles and attitudes of the travellers break down under the impact of the wilderness. Those travellers who are able to transcend their former roles are regenerated by the experience: the drunken doctor delivers a baby, the meek salesman shows courage, the whore becomes the heroine of a romance and the outlaw becomes a lover. By stunning photographic representation of the visual contrasts of desert, hills and moving stagecoach, Ford transforms the journey of the stagecoach into an epic voyage that transcends the film's rather limited romantic plot.

Costume—another feature of the Western setting—has also contributed greatly to the Western's success in film. Like topography, Western costume gains effectiveness both from intrinsic interest and from the way writers and filmmakers have learned how to make it reflect character and theme. In simplest form, as in the B Westerns, costumes symbolized moral opposition. The good guy wore clean, well-pressed clothes and a white hat. The villain dressed sloppily in black. The importance of this convention, simple-minded as it was, became apparent when, to create a more sophisticated "adult"

Western, directors frequently chose to dress their heroes in black. However, the tradition of western costume also contains more complex meanings. An important distinction marks off both hero and villain from the townspeople. The townspeople usually wear the ordinary street clothing associated with the later nineteenth century, suits for men and long dresses for women. On the whole this clothing is simple as compared to the more elaborate fashions of the period and this simplicity is one way of expressing the Westernness of the costume. However, in the midst of the desert, the townspeople's clothing has an air of non-utilitarian artificiality somewhat like the ubiquitous false fronts on the town itself. It is perhaps significant that even in Westerns purportedly set at a later date, the women tend to wear the full-length dresses of an earlier period.

The costumes associated with heroes and outlaws or savages are more striking. Paradoxically they are both more utilitarian and more artificial than those of the townspeople. The cowboy's boots, tight-fitting pants or chaps, his heavy shirt and bandana, his gun and finally his ten-gallon hat all symbolize his adaptation to the wilderness. But utility is only one of the principles of the hero-outlaw's dress. The other is dandyism, that highly artificial love of elegance for its own sake. In the Western, dandyism sometimes takes the overt and obvious form of elaborate costumes laid over with fringes, tassels and scrollwork like a rococo drawing room. But it is more powerfully exemplified in the elegance of those beautifully tailored cowboy uniforms which John Wayne so magnificently fills out in the Westerns of John Ford and Howard Hawks.

The enormous attraction of this combination of naturalness and artifice has played a significant role in both popular and avant-garde art since the middle of the nineteenth century. Beaudelaire's fascination with the dandyism of the savage which he described as "the supreme incarnation of the idea of Beauty transported into the material world," is just one indication of the nineteenth century's fascination with the mixture of savagery and elegance which has been implicit in the costume of the Western hero from the beginning. Cooper's Leatherstocking even gained his name from his costume, suggesting the extent to which this particular kind of dress excited Cooper's imagination. Like later cowboys, Leatherstocking's costume combined nature and artifice. His dress was largely made of the skins of animals and it was particularly adapted to the needs of wilderness life. Yet at the same time it was subtly ornamented with buckskin fringes and procupine quills "after the manner of the Indians." Still it is important to note that Leatherstock's costume is not that of the Indians, but rather a more utilitarian wilderness version of the settler's dress. Thus, costume exemplified the mediating role of the hero between civilization and savagery. Later the formula cowboy's costume developed along the same lines. In its basic outlines it resembled town dress more than that of the Indian, yet it was more functional for movement across the plains than that of the townspeople. At the same time, the cowboy dress had a dandyish splendor and elegance lacking in the drab fashions of the town and based on Indian or Mexican models. In later Westerns, the hero shared many of these qualities with the villain, just as Leatherstocking had a touch of the Indian, despite his repeated assurances that he was "a man without a cross," i.e., actual Indian kinship. But the hero's costume still differentiated him from the savage, whether Indian or outlaw, both by its basic resemblance to civilized dress and by its greater restraint and decorum. Thus costume, like setting, expressed the transcendent and intermediate quality of the hero. By lying between two ways of life, he transcended the restrictions and limitations of both. Or, to put it another way, the Western setting and costume embody the basic escapist principle of having your cake and eating it too.

2)   Complex of Characters

As already indicated, there are three central roles in the Western: the townspeople or agents of civilization, the savages or outlaws who threaten this first group, and the heroes who are above all "men in the middle," that is, they possess many qualities and skills of the savages but are fundamentally committed to the townspeople. It is out of the multiple variations possible on the relationships between these groups that the various Western plots are concocted. For example, the simplest version of all has the hero protecting the townspeople from the savages, using his own savage skills against the denizens of the wilderness. A second more complex variation shows the hero initially indifferent to the plight of the townspeople and more inclined to identify himself with the savages. However, in the course of the story his position changes and he becomes the ally of the townspeople. This variation can generate a number of different plots. There is the revenge Western: a hero seeks revenge against an outlaw or Indian who has wronged him. In order to accomplish his vengeance, he rejects the pacifistic ideals of the townspeole, but in the end he discovers that he is really committed to their way of life (John Ford's *The Searchers*). Another plot based on this variation of the character relations is that of the hero who initially seeks his own selfish material gain, using his savage skills as a means to his end; but, as the story progresses, he discovers his moral involvement with the townspeople and becomes their champion (cf. Anthony Mann's film *The Far Country*). It is also possible, while maintaining the system of relationships, to reverse the conclusion of the plot as in those stories where the townspeople come to accept the hero's savage mode of action (cf. John Ford's *Stagecoach* or, to a certain extent, Wister's *The Virginian*). A third variation of the basic scheme of relationships has the hero caught in the middle between the townspeople's need for his savage skills and their rejection of his way of life. This third variation, common in recent Westerns, often ends in the destruction of the hero (cf. the films *The Gunfighter* or *Invitation to a Gunfighter*) or in his voluntary exile (*Shane, High Noon, Two Rode Together*). The existence of these and many other variations suggest that the exploration of a certain pattern of relationships is more important to the Western than a particular outcome, though it is also probable that they reflect different components of the mass audience, the simpler variation being more popular with the adolescents and the more complex variations successful with adults. In addition, changing cultural attitudes have something to do with the emergence of different variations, since variation two is clearly more characteristic of early twentieth century Westerns, while variation three dominates the recent "adult" Western.

The most important single fact about the group of townspeople is that there are women in it. Character groupings in the Western often show a dual as well as tripartite opposition: the hero and the savages are men while the town is strongly dominated by women. This sexual division frequently embodies the antithesis of civilization and savagery. Women are primary symbols of civilization in the Western. It is the schoolmarm even more than the entrepreneur who signals the end of the old wilderness life. Women are also women, however, and implicit in their presence is the sexual fascination and fear associated with the rape of white women by savages. Though few Westerns explicitly develop this theme and many writers even try to deny its place in their narratives, there seems little doubt that the possible savage capture of women plays a crucial role in many Westerns and an implicit role in most. Leslie Fiedler has done the most interesting work in analyzing the psychological undercurrents of the curious Western triangle between hero, savage and female. His interpretation stresses the strong emotional, cultural and even sexual ties between hero and savage which are threatened and finally disrupted by the female. He concludes that the violence endemic to this triangle reflects the terrible incompatibility between the free spontaneity and sexuality associated with savagery and the genteel restrictiveness of civilized monogamous domesticity. Thus, Fiedler interprets the Western as a popular myth embodying the psychological tensions which Freud describes in *Civilization and its Discontents*. Civilization represses spontaneous sexuality and creates a growing neurotic obsession with death and destruction. The hero's destruction of the savage in order to protect the chastity of the schoolmarm symbolizes the repression of his own spontaneous sexual urges and his acceptance of the monogamous sexual pattern of modern middle-class life.

Further evidence for the significance of this Western triangle lies in the frequent presence of two different kinds of women in the Western. This dichotomy resembles the common nineteenth century novelistic dualism of blonde and brunette. The blonde, like Cooper's Alice in *The Last of the Mohicans*, represents, genteel, pure femininity, while the brunette, like

Cora in the same novel, symbolizes a more full-blooded, passionate and spontaneous nature, often slightly tainted by a mixture of blood or a dubious past. In the contemporary Western, this feminine duality shows up in the contrast between the schoolmarm and the dance-hall girl, or between the hero's Mexican or Indian mistress and the WASP girl he may ultimately marry. The dark girl is a feminine embodiment of the hero's savage, spontaneous side. She understands his deep passions, his savage code of honor and his need to use personal violence. The schoolmarm's civilized code of behavior rejects the passionate urges and the freedom of aggression which mark this side of the hero's character. When the hero becomes involved with the schoolmarm, the dark lady must be destroyed or abandoned, just as Cooper's Cora must die because her feelings are too passionate and spontaneous to be viable in the genteel world of Alice and Duncan Heyward. Even when the relationship between the hero and the dance-hall girl seems to be permanent and almost domestic, like the long-standing friendship between Kitty and Marshal Dillon on the TV series *Gunsmoke*, it typically remains in suspension and never leads to marriage.

With women as central agents, the town reflects a somewhat ambiguous view of the values of civilization, an ambiguity which is invariably resolved in favor of social progress, but not without some reluctance and sense of loss. The town offers love, domesticity and order as well as the opportunity for personal achievement and the creation of a family, but it requires the repression of spontaneous passion and the curtailment of the masculine honor and camaraderie of the older wilderness life. These ambiguities are reflected in the hero's relationship with women. They are also embodied in the three main kinds of townspeople who recurrently appear in Westerns: the pioneers or decent folk, the escapees from civilization and the banker-villains. The pioneers resemble the hero in being virtuous and honorable people, but they lack his ability to cope with savagery. In addition, their aims are fundamentally different. The hero's primary moral concern is to preserve himself with individual dignity and honor in a savage and violent environment. The pioneers represent a collective force which seeks to transform the wilderness into a new social order. Their values center around the establishment of stable families and the building of homes, farms and businesses. Instead of individual honor, they value hard work, mutual loyalty and political and economic achievement; in short, the conventional American canons of success. Typically, much of the action of the Western centers around the initial mixture of conflict and sympathy between hero and pioneers, which eventually resolves itself into the hero's commitment to the cause of the pioneers. Sometimes the commitment is happy in its outcome as in Wister's *The Virginian*, where the hero is able to synthesize his personal code with the morality of the pioneers and become a successful rancher and political leader. In other cases, the conflict cannot be overcome and the hero's commitment becomes sacrifical. Such was the result of the relation between Judge Temple and Natty Bumppo in Cooper's *The Pioneers*, though in that novel a synthesis between hero and pioneers was attempted in the figure of Oliver Effingham. The sacrificial outcome also characterizes most of the significant recent Westerns. In Jack Schaefer's *Shane* the hero becomes involved with pioneer Joe Starrett. Throughout the first part of the book we are shown the mixture of mutual sympathy and conflict which characterizes the relationship of two men of equal virtue but different aims and codes. Finally, Shane's commitment to the pioneer cause forces him to reenact his role as a gunman. But, as a killer, he can no longer remain a part of the pioneer community. Wounded in his battle for the pioneers he must ride off into the wilderness again. A similar pattern dominates John Ford's film *The Man Who Shot Liberty Valance*. The hero, Tom Doniphon, must sacrifice himself and his way of life to save the pioneer leader who will be instrumental in destroying the older anarchal society which is the only real background for the hero.

A second group of townspeople, who have become particularly prominent in more recent Westerns, combines in single individuals some of the ambiguities of civilization which appear in the conflict between hero and pioneers. This group consists of people who have fled the East. For them the West is not a place to build up a new civilization but a haven from failure or personal tragedy in the East. The masculine form of this figure is commonly the drunken professional, particularly a doctor or a lawyer who, we are given to understand, had a promising Eastern career which went sour. The female type is the dance-hall girl who, like the drunken professional, has had some shattering experience in the East and has come West to lick her wounds. These figures are commonly alienated from the rest of the townspeople and consequently are better able to understand the hero's moral imperatives. Yet they cannot function on the hero's ground either since they lack his skills in violence or his strong sense of honor. They often play one or more of three important plot roles: first, they provide sympathy and even assistance to the hero at a crucial time; second, they are better able to initiate the reluctant hero into the virtues represented by the pioneers since they share some of the hero's ambiguity and yet remain basically committed to the town; finally, a savage attack on one of these figures often provides the final push behind the hero's commitment to the cause of the pioneers. In *The Man Who Shot Liberty Valance* it is the savage outlaw's vicious attack on the drunken professional that finally convinces Tom Doniphon of the necessity of playing a role on the side of the pioneers.

Thematically the escapee from civilization seems to be a means of expressing both some sense of the limitations of civilization and yet of reaffirming what the town stands for. The escapee gains our sympathy and that of the hero by his alienation and failure. Yet from this very position of alienation and failure, he represents the limitations of individualism and the ultimate necessity of commitment to the town, for he, like the hero, discovers that he cannot maintain his prideful isolation when the chips are down and the savage attack has begun. In addition, the escapee serves as an important foil to the hero. His garrulous weakness sets off the hero's silent strength, his enforced alienation and failure contrast with the hero's voluntary isolation and pride. Moreover, his very presence is a testimony to the failure of society to provide an honorable and meaningful role for some of its choice spirits, thus enhancing our sympathy for the hero's own initial alienation from society.

The escapee mediates between the hero and the town and

in doing so represents some of the ambiguous feelings toward society which the Western embodies. A third type of town figure symbolizes the negative side of civilization. This is the unscrupulous banker, rancher or railroad agent who sometimes plays the role of central villain by becoming the employer or manipulator of the Indians or outlaws who actually perform the acts of savagery. This figure represents the decent ideals of the pioneer gone sour. In him the pioneer goal of building a good society in the wilderness has become avarice and greed for individual wealth and power. Instead of the pioneer's mutual respect and loyalty, the banker-villain possesses skill at manipulating and exploiting the townspeople to his own advantage. This figure appears as the tyrannical rancher Luke Fletcher in Schaefer's *Shane*, as the grasping banker in Richard Wilson's *Invitation to a Gunfighter*, as both the evil gambler Durade and the avaricious capitalist Lee in Zane Grey's *The U.P. Trail*. Sometimes he is the unscrupulous Indian agent who makes corrupt bargains with Indians on the warpath, or the mortgage foreclosder who drives the romanticized outlaw into a life of crime. It is tempting to say that in the twentieth century this townsman-villain has increasingly usurped the traditional role of the savage as villain, but this would be an overstatement, for the banker-villain was implicit in the Western from the beginning. In *The Pioneers* Cooper clearly adumbrated him in the scheming lawyer Hiram Doolittle and the greedy miner Jotham Riddle. In the dime novel, this character was a favorite villain. Characters like Hon. Cecil Grosvenor of *Deadwood Dick on Deck* resemble one of the recurrent adversaries in the Horatio Alger stories, the greedy squire or avaricious relative who seeks to exploit the Alger hero by keeping him in a servile position, but whose plot is foiled when the hero makes contact with the benevolent merchant (the analogue to the pioneers in the Alger stories). However, this character does play a more prominent role in the twentieth century and his greater importance reflects the changing thematic content of the Western.

The second major character role in the Western is that of the savage. In his simplest form the savage is the bloodthirsty Indian or lawless outlaw who is the irreconcilable adversary of hero and townspeople. While some Westerns do not get much beyond the simple opposition of good hero and evil savages, the relationship is rather more complex in most examples of the formula. The savages are not invariably villains, for, beginning with Cooper the idea of the noble savage played an important role in the tradition of the Western manifesting itself variously in virtuous Indians and "good" outlaws who exist in complex counterpoint with the evil savages. This double view of the savage mirrors the double meaning of wilderness on which I have already commented. The presence of both noble and diabolical manifestations of savagery reflects the same kind of ambiguity about the progress of civilization which I noted in discussing the townspeople. The savage symbolizes the violence, brutality and ignorance which civilized society seeks to control and eliminate, but he also commonly stands for certain positive values which are restricted or destroyed by advancing civilization: the freedom and spontaneity of wilderness life, the sense of personal honor and individual mastery, and the deep camaraderie of men untrammelled by domestic ties. In both his roles it turns out that the savage must be destroyed but in one case we rejoice and in the other feel nostalgically sorry. Two major modes of the Western derive from this distinction. There is the comic-heroic in novels like Wister's *The Virginian*, where the hero destroys the bad savages and achieves a synthesis between noble savagery and civilization in his own person. The second major mode is that of the elegiac which dominates the novels of Cooper and many recent Westerns. Here the imperatives of civilization and the good values of savagery prove irreconcilable and we are invited to lament the passing of these values as the price which must be paid for civilization.

It is possible to have Westerns without Indians or outlaws, but not without somebody playing the role of savage, for the antithesis between townspeople and savagery is the source of plots. Frequently we have a character who changes from savage to hero in the course of the story. For example, in John Ford's *Three Godfathers*, the three central characters are wild outlaws in flight from the law at the beginning of the film. Fleeing across the desert they come upon a lost woman who gives birth to a child and then dies after having made the three outlaws promise to care for the baby. Accepting this responsibility changes the outlaws from savages into heroes by placing them in that typical posture of the Western hero: a situation of divided commitment. As outlaws they are committed to battling with the law, as godfathers to the peaceful domesticity of civilization. In resolving this conflict the film makes use of the comic-heroic mode of the Western. Two of the outlaws are killed while heroically struggling to bring the child safely across the desert. The third arrives in "New Jerusalem" where he refuses to give the child to anyone else for adoption, even though the judge tempts him with a suspended sentence. This proof of a basic commitment to domesticity enables the judge to mete out a minimal sentence and the movie ends happily with the whole town turned out to see the outlaw-hero off to prison.

As I have already noted, the role of savage can be played interchangeably by Indians or outlaws because both groups symbolize the same basic qualities: negativity, lawlessness, a love of violence, rejection of the town and its way of life, and, more positively, the capacity to live and move freely in the wilderness, mastery of the tools of violence and strong masculinity. Insofar as the Western writer chooses to emphasize the villainous qualities of the savage it is primarily through his ruthless violence. When the writer wishes to present the nobility of savagery, he usually stresses the savage's code of personal honor and his complete physical courage in defending his honor, those qualities which relate him to the hero. In the twentieth century Western, the outlaw has increasingly taken over the role of the "bad" savage, while the Indian seems more and more to embody the positive virtues of savagery. This reverses a relation common in the nineteenth century dime novel in which the outlaw was often romanticized as a noble outcast and the Indian treated as a diabolical villain.

Another important aspect in the treatment of savagery in the Western formula is its relation to madness. Cooper sometimes used this device to distinguish between his noble and vicious savages. Thus, in *The Last of the Mohicans* the noble savages Uncas and Chingachgook can be as bloodthirsty as the villainous Mingos but still be sharply differentiated because the noble savages are motivated by a code of personal honor, while the diabolical Magua, their adversary, is obsessed with a mad desire for power and vengeance. The symbolic role of madness has flickered in and out of the Western throughout its history attaching itself to such varied figures as the nineteenth century "Indian-hater" and the psychotic outlaw of the recent adult Western. In general, its function seems to be one of distinguishing between the hero's disciplined and moral use of violence and the uncontrollable aggression which marks the "bad" savage. It is also likely that there is some relation between the idea of savagery that marks the Westerns. For both madness and savagery are forms of reaction against the lawful order of the town.

In the simplest Westerns, the townspeople and the savages represent a basic moral opposition between good and evil. In most examples of the formula, however, the opposition is a more complex one, a dialectic of contrasting ways of life or psychic states. The resolution of this opposition is the work of the hero. Thus the most basic definition of the hero role in the Western is as the figure who resolves the conflict between pioneers and savages. Because there is a considerable range of complexity in the definition of this conflict, there is also a considerable range in the characterization of the hero. Thus the Western hero might be classified along a scale which runs from Hopalong Cassidy and the Lone Ranger to much more complex figures like Cooper's Natty Bumppo, Jimmy Ringo of Henry King's *The Gunfighter* and Tom Doniphon of John Ford's *The Man Who Shot Liberty Valance*. The Hopalong Cassidy-Lone Ranger figure is a character of minimal ambiguity. He is supremely good and masterful in his skills. His commitment to the pioneer cause creates no inner conflict, even though this kind of Western does often employ a simple device like the seeming outlawry of the Lone Ranger and Deadwood Dick to cast a mythical aura about the hero. This hero's difficulties spring primarily from the plots of the unregenerate savages and banker-villains who are his and the pioneers' adversaries. In the end these problems are resolved by a dazzling display of the hero's virtuosity in violence as in the climactic scene of *Hopalong Cassidy and the Forty*

Thieves, where Hoppy shoots it out with a town full of outlaws and emerges victorious.

At the other end of the scale, the hero is a more complex figure because he has internalized the conflict between savagery and civilization. His inner conflict between the new values of civilization and the personal heroism and honor of the old wilderness tends to overshadow the clash between savages and townspeople. While he undertakes to protect and save the pioneers, this type of hero also senses that his own feelings and his special quality as a hero are bound up with the wilderness life. The outcome of Westerns which present this version of the hero are invariably more ambiguous and tragic. If we look for mythical archetypes for the Western hero, we might compare the Lone Ranger type with Perseus or Bellerophon, dragon-slaying bravos who have been provided with magical steeds and other aids by the gods and whose problems in accomplishing their missions are purely strategic or technological. Once they have managed to acquire the appropriate silver bullets or magic helmets they are able to move directly and without ambiguity to the destruction of the savage monster.

The archetype of the more complex Western hero would have to be Achilleus, that great warrior torn between his loyalty to the Achaeans and his transcendent sense of personal honor. When he is finally drawn into the conflict that will destroy him, his former joy in violence and war become a bitter and resigned acceptance of fate. As I have already observed, this more complex Western hero is rather more elegiac than tragic and he does not reach the profound depths of grief and knowledge that Achilleus does, but the similarity is unmistakable.

If we ask why the Western hero, despite his resemblance to Achilleus, does not reach anything like the tragic magnitude of that figure, we are led to another insight into the nature of popular formula stories. The tragic power of Achilleus' predicament lies in the degree to which it forces us to confront the inescapable mystery of life, the terrible limitations of the human desire for immortality and the inextricable relation between glory and death. The predicament of Achilleus embodies these paradoxes in the most overpowering and universal terms. In the Western story, however, the hero's situation is linked to a particular period of history with its limited way of life. It would be absurd to think that Achilleus' problem would be resolved by a change in social conditions, just as it would be silly to say that Hamlet might have lived happily ever after if he could only have availed himself of the services of a good psychoanalyst. But this is more or less the way we are made to see the Western hero. Insofar as he is the embodiment of a particular moment in history his failure or tragedy can make us sad, but it does not forcibly bring us face to face with ourselves and our present life. In the destruction of the gunfighter or the sad departure of Shane, we lament the hero's fate, and we feel nostalgic about the passing of a time when men were men, but at the same time we see their sacrifice as a necessary contribution to progress. And besides even in losing they have been victorious over the villain. Their fate is not ours. Nonetheless, of all the popular action-adventure formulas, the Western is the one which sometimes comes closest to tragedy.

Between the eternally victorious Lone Ranger and the more ambiguous and tragic gunfighter, there exists a whole range of Western heroes more complex than the masked rider but less tragic than the gunfighter. Two types dominate this comic-heroic area of our scale of Western heroes and they are mirror images of each other. The first is the wild cowboy who becomes a pioneer leader, frequently by marrying the schoolmarm. The classic embodiment of this hero is Wister's *The Virginian*. The second type is a dude come West who duplicates the metamorphosis of the cowboy into a pioneer in reverse. This hero starts out as an easterner, usually a very aristocratic one. He has come West because he feels that his way of life has become corrupt and decadent; he seeks regeneration in the great, open spaces. Gradually, he becomes an initiate of the Code of the West, and by the end of the story he has become a cowboy of cowboys. This version of the hero can be found in such novels as Harold Bell Wright's *When a Man's a Man*, and in many of the stories of Zane Grey. He is of particular cultural interest because he was partly inspired by the actual western odysseys of a number of prominent eastern aristocrats like Theodore Roosevelt and Frederic Remington at the end of the nineteenth century.[20]

The hero is a man with a horse and the horse is his direct tie to the freedom of the wilderness, for it embodies his ability to move freely across it and to dominate and control its spirit. Through the intensity of his relationship to his horse, the cowboy excites that human fantasy of unity with natural creatures—the same fantasy seen in such figures as the centaurs of Greek mythology, in Siegfried's ability to understand the language of birds and in a hero whose popularity was contemporaneous with the flourishing of the Western: Tarzan of the Apes.

The Western hero is also a man with a gun. The interaction of American attitudes toward violence and the image of the Western gunfighter is so complex that it seems impossible to determine which causes the other. Critics of violence in the mass media believe that the heroic romanticized violence of the Western hero is a dangerous model for young people and stimulates them to imitation of the man with the gun. Defenders of the mass media argue that Westerns and other violent adventure dramas simply reflect the culture's fascination with guns. There have been many investigations of violence in the mass media and a large-scale government inquiry has recently been undertaken. Insofar as it seeks to determine the causal role of the Western hero in fostering violence among those who follow his adventures, this inquiry will probably be as inconclusive as the rest, for in my opinion both the tendency to admire gunfighter heroes and the actual social incidence of violence with guns are both symptoms of a more complex cultural force: the sense of decaying masculine potency which has long afflicted American culture. The American obsession with masculinity so often observed by Europeans and so evident in every aspect of our culture from serious artists like Ernest Hemingway to the immense range of gutsy men's magazines, *Playboy* images, and mass sports reflect a number of major social trends which undercut the sense of male security. Among the most important of these developments is the tendency of industrial work to depend increasingly on the superior potency of machines, the increasing importance of women in the industrial economy, the nationalizing trend of American life which has eroded local communities and the individual's sense of control over his life and finally the decline of parental authority in the family which has undercut the basic source of masculine supremacy. Yet, at the same time, the American tradition has always emphasized individual masculine force; Americans love to think of themselves as pioneers, men who have conquered a continent and sired on it a new society. This radical discrepancy between the sense of eroding masculinity and the view of America as a great history of men against the wilderness has created the need for a means of symbolic expression of masculine potency in an unmistakable way. This means the gun, particularly the six-gun.

Walter Prescott Webb suggests that the development of Colt's revolver was the critical invention that made possible the American assault on the Great Plains. As Webb sees it, the Plains Indians with their horses and their extraordinary skill with the bow and arrow had a mobility and firepower unequalled until the adoption of the six-gun by the Texas Rangers. From that point on the Americans had a military advantage over the Plains Indians and the rapid development of the "Cattle Kingdom" followed. The historical and cultural significance of the gun as the means by which the cowboy drove out the Indian inhabitants of the plains shaped a new culture happened to coincide with the long-standing tradition of heroism and masculine honor, that of the medieval knight, and its later offshoot, the code of the duel. For the Westerner's six-gun and his way of using it in individual combat was the closest thing in the armory of modern violence to the knight's sword and the duellist's pistol. Thus in a period when violence in war was becoming increasingly anonymous and incomprehensible with massed attacks and artillery duels accounting for most of the casualties, the cowboy hero in his isolated combat with Indian or outlaw seemed to reaffirm the traditional image of masculine strength, honor and moral violence. The cowboy hero with his six-gun standing between the uncontrolled violence of the savages and the evolving collective forces of the legal process played out in new terms the older image of chivalrous adventure. Not surprisingly an age which so enjoyed the historical romances of Sir Walter Scott would color the cowboy with tints freely borrowed from *Ivanhoe* and *Rob Roy*.

Many critics of the Western have commented upon the gun as a phallic symbol, suggesting that the firing of the gun symbolizes the moment of ejaculation in a sexual act. Insofar as this is the case it bears out the emphasis on masculine potency already noted. However, this kind of phallic symbolism is an almost universal property of adventure heroes. The knight has his sword, the hard-boiled detective his automatic pistol, Buck Rogers his ray gun. The distinctive characteristic of the cowboy hero is not his possession of a symbolic weapon but the way in which he uses it.

While the knight encountered his adversary in bloody hand-to-hand combat, the cowboy invariably meets his at a substantial distance and goes through the complex and rigid ritual of the "draw" before finally consummating the fatal deed. The most important implication of this killing procedure seems to be the qualities of reluctance, control and elegance which it associates with the hero. Unlike the knight, the cowboy hero does not seek out combat for its own sake and he typically shows an aversion to the wanton shedding of blood. Killing is an act forced upon him and he carries it out with the precision and skill of a surgeon and the careful proportions of an artist. We might say that the six-gun is that weapon which enables the hero to show the largest measure of objectivity and detachment while yet engaging in individual combat. This controlled and aesthetic mode of killing is particularly important as the supreme mark of differentiation between the hero and the savage. The Indian or outlaw as savage delights in slaughter, entering into combat with a kind of manic glee to fulfill an uncontrolled lust for blood. The hero never engages in violence until the last moment and he never kills until the savage's gun has already cleared his holster. Suddenly it is there and the villain crumples.

This peculiar emphasis on the hero's skilled and detached killing from a distance has been a part of the Western since its inception. One thinks, for example, of that climactic scene in *The Last of the Mohicans* where Leatherstocking picks the villainous Magua off the cliff top with a single shot from his unerring long rifle. The cowboy hero fights in a little closer within the smaller range of the six-gun, but the same basic pattern of individual combat at a distance with the hero's last minute precision and control defeating the villain's undisciplined and savage aggression is the same. Careful staging of the final duel with all its elaborate protocol became a high point of the film Western, another example of an element of the literary Western which turned out to have even greater potential for the film.

The hero often fights with his fists, but he never kills in this kind of direct hand-to-hand combat. Moreover, he rarely uses any weapon other than his fists, since knives and clubs suggest a more aggressive uncontrolled kind of violence which seems instinctively wrong for the character of the cowboy hero. Thus, the hero's special skill at gunfighting not only symbolizes his masculine potency, but indicates that his violence is disciplined and pure.

Something like the old ideal of knightly purity and chastity survives in the cowboy hero's basic aversion to the grosser and dirtier forms of violence. In addition, the hero's reluctant but aesthetic approach to killing seems to reflect the ambiguity about violence which pervades modern society. Twentieth century America is perhaps the most ideologically pacifistic nation in history. Its political and social values are anti-militaristic, its legal ideals reject personal violence and it sees itself as a nation dedicated to world peace and domestic harmony through law and order. Yet this same nation supports one of the largest military establishments in history, its rate of violent crimes is enormously high and it possesses the technological capacity to destroy the world. Perhaps one source of the cowboy hero's appeal is the way in which he resolves this ambiguity by giving a sense of moral significance and order to violence. His reluctance and detachment, the way in which he kills only when he is forced to do so, the aesthetic order he imposes upon his acts of violence through the abstract ritual of the shootdown, and finally his mode of killing cleanly and purely at a distance through the magic of his six-gun cover the nakedness of violence and aggression beneath a skin of aesthetic and moral propriety.

Certain other characteristics are connected with the hero's role as middleman between the pacifistic townspeople and the violent savages. There is his oft-noted laconic style, for example. Not all Western heroes are tight-lipped strong, silent types. Some, like Leatherstocking, are downright garrulous.

But the laconic style is commonly associated with the Western hero, particularly in the twentieth century when movie stars like Gary Cooper, John Wayne, James Stewart and Henry Fonda have vied for the prize as the Western hero who can say the fewest words with the least expression. Actually tight lips are far more appropriate to the formula hero than the torrent of didacticism which flows from the lips of Natty Bumppo, and which most readers of Cooper resolutely ignore. Like his gun, language is a weapon the hero rarely uses, but when he does, it is with precise and powerful effectiveness. In addition, the hero's reluctance with language reflects his social isolation and his reluctance to commit himself to the action which he knows will invariably lead to another violent confrontation.

Reluctance with words often matches the hero's reluctance toward women. Cooper's Leatherstocking marked out one basic course the Western hero would take with respect to the fair sex. The one girl Natty falls in love with, Mabel Dunham in *The Pathfinder*, is too young and civilized to return his love and he gives her up to the younger, less wilderness-loving Jasper Western. On the other hand, the girl who falls in love with Natty, Judith Hutter in *The Deerslayer*, is too wild and too passionate to capture the affection of the chaste and pure Leatherstocking. This romantic situation reflects Natty's position as a man who mediates between civilization and wildness. Cooper found it increasingly difficult to resolve this antithesis and Natty remained caught in the middle between his loved forest and the oncoming civilization which he had served. At other periods, writers have tried to make a romantic hero out of the cowboy, as in Wister's *The Virginian* and the many novels of Zane Grey. However, even when the hero does get the girl, the clash between the hero's adherence to the "Code of the West" and the heroine's commitment to domesticity, social success or other genteel values usually plays a role in the story. Heroes such as the Lone Ranger tend to avoid romance altogether. They are occasionally pursued by women but generally manage to evade their clutches.

The hero's true social milieu, until he is transformed by the commitment to civilization forced on him in the course of the story, is the group of masculine comrades, the boys at the ranch, the other horse soldiers or the Indian sidekicks. However much he may be alienated from the town, the Western hero almost never appears without some kind of membership in a group of males. Often the group of comrades represents a marginal or alienated social class with an ethnic or national background different from that of the hero: the WASP cavalry officer has his Irish sergeant, the cowboy has his Indian, Mexican and in some recent Westerns his Negro companions. Leslie Fiedler has pointed out how the theme of good companionship between outcast white and men of darker skin plays a complex role in American literature, pointing to such examples as Cooper's Natty Bumppo and his Indian friend Chingachgook, Melville's Ishmael and the South Sea Islander Queequeg, Mark Twain's Huck Finn and Jim, Faulkner's Ike McCaslin and Sam Fathers. Fiedler argues that this relationship "symbolically joins the white man to nature and his own unconscious . . . and binds him in life-long loyalty to a help-meet, without the sacrifice of his freedom. This is the pure marriage of males—sexless and holy, a kind of counter-matrimony, in which the white refugee from society and the dark-skinned primitive are joined till death do them part."[21] According to Fiedler, this theme is an implicit attack on middle-class ideals of gentility, success and domesticity which repress natural instincts and consequently threaten masculine identity. As we have seen, the concern for masculine potency and the representation of a conflict between civilized order and savage freedom also play a vital role in the Western. However, the formula Western usually attempts to resolve this conflict and to evade some of its deeper implications. While there are Westerns in which the hero remains an outcast, it is more usual for him to move from the milieu of the masculine comrade into a commitment to the town and even into a romance. Moreover, while certain important Western heroes like the Lone Ranger retain the original companion theme, in the majority of Westerns the dark-skinned comrade is replaced by the boys at the ranch, muting the racial significance of the symbolism.

However, though the formula Western may evade the racial or radical undertones which Fiedler sees as typical of the treatment of masculine comradeship in American literature, association with the boys remains one of the most important aspects of the hero's life and style. Not only do the hero's ties of friendship motivate much of his behavior, but in most cases the great sense of honor and adherence to a highly disciplined code of behavior which sharply differentiates hero from savages and outlaws springs from his association with the masculine group. The "Code of the West" is in every respect a male ethic and its values and prescriptions relate primarily to the relationships of men. In theory the code prescribes a role for women as an adjunct to masculine honor. Nevertheless the presence of women invariably threatens the primacy of the masculine group. In many Westerns an interesting resolution of this conflict is worked out. The woman in effect takes over the role of the masculine comrades and becomes the hero's true companion. A good example of this is the case of the heroine Georgianna Stockwell of Zane Grey's *The Code of the West*. When she comes West, Georgiana is a flapper and her promiscuity in word, though not in deed, sets her in complete opposition to the "Code." After nearly destroying young Cal Thurman, who falls in love with her, Georgianna realizes that her moral outlook has been wrong and that she has herself fallen in love with the simple but dedicated Cal. Once this transformation has taken place, the false eastern sophistication which placed Georgianna in opposition to the "Code" gives way and the strength of her new character enables her to confront the villain who threatens to kill her wounded husband. In effect Georgianna Stockwell becomes one of the boys herself and her final confrontation with Bid Hatfield takes the place of the usual shootdown. While this is an extreme form of the transformation of the female heroine from a threat to masculine identity into a true comrade, the theme is a common one in those Westerns where the hero plays a romantic role as well as his basic one of ambiguous defender of the town.

The hero's membership in the masculine gang and his initial rejection of domesticity relates to another trait he commonly possesses: his desire to keep moving. Just as Natty Bumppo felt he had to move on when the settlers's cabins began to impinge on his wilderness, so the modern cowboy hero is represented as a bit of a drifter. As one of his pals tells the hero in Ernest Haycox's *The Man in the Saddle*: "That's your trouble. Always goin' off to take another look at a piece of country. Fiddle-footed. Always smellin' the wind for scent. And so you lose out."[22] This quotation neatly sums up the cowboy hero's instinctive rejection of the ethic of success at least in the early stages of the story. The cowboy hero is far from a hero of work and enterprise. Indeed he is rarely represented as working at all. Nonetheless, the formula requires that the hero somehow possess the necessary funds to maintain himself in horses, food, ammunition and elegant costumes, though it is rarely clear just where or how he gets this money. When one reads a more or less realistic narrative of cowboy life such as Andy Adams' *Log of a Cowboy* or looks at actual photographs of cowboys in action such as those of Erwin Smith, the thing that stands out most strikingly in comparison to the formula Western is the amount of hard, dirty physical labor involved. As Robert Warshow puts it, "the Westerner is *par excellence* a man of leisure. Even when he wears the badge of a marshal or, more rarely, owns a ranch, he appears to be unemployed." Thus, in many respects the cowboy hero represents an image of man directly opposed to the official American pioneer virtues of progress, success and domesticity. In place of "getting ahead" he pursues the ideal of honor which he shares with his masculine comrades. Warshow neatly summarizes this aspect of the hero's character:

he fights not for advantage and not for the right, but to state what he is, and he must live in a world which permits that statement. The Westerner is the last gentleman and the movies which over and over tell his story are probably the last art form in which the concept of honor retains its strength.[23]

Even in this case, however, the tendency of popular formulas is to seek for a resolution of thematic conflicts or to evade them altogether. Few Westerns carry the antithesis between success and honor to its inevitable conclusion: the destruction or exile of the hero from the developing town which can no longer permit the explosions of individual will and aggression necessary to the defense of heroic honor.

More typically a way is found in the course of the action to reconcile hero and town and to assimilate the cowboy hero into the world of the pioneers. There are innumerable plot devices which perform this function. The hero falls in love and thus becomes ultimately committed to the pioneer cause. The woman falls in love with the hero and her dedication to him enables her to take over the role of the true male companions.

Or the hero simply becomes old and tired and decides that it is finally time to settle down. Different periods in the history of the Western have preferred different kinds of resolutions. For example, the early twentieth century clearly preferred to solve the clash of values through romance, while more recent Westerns have made a great deal of the tired hero who reluctantly gives up the heroic way of life either because he accepts the necessity of civilization or because he is tired of insecurity. The tired hero often shades over into the sacrificial hero who accepts death or exile because he cannot work out the conflict between the town and his heroic past. It is in treating this version of the Western hero that the formula Western commonly reaches its most moving and significant level as art, a quality which Warshow brilliantly defines in his essay on the Western hero:

The Westerner is a ... classical figure, self-contained and limited to begin with, seeking not to extend his domination but only to assert his personal value, and his tragedy lies in the fact that even this circumscribed demand cannot be fully realized. Since the Westerner is not a murderer but (most of the time) a man of virtue, and since he is always prepared for defeat, he retains his inner invulnerability and his story need not end with his death (and usually does not); but what we finally respond to is not his victory but his defeat.[24]

3)   Types of Situations and Patterns of Action

As these remarks on the variety of hero-types indicate there is a great variety of situations and plots that can be made into Westerns as long as the basic conventions of setting and character relations are maintained. Thus our treatment of situation and pattern of action can be very general and brief here. There is a kind of basic situation which various Western plots tend to embody which I have already defined in my discussion of setting and characters. Basically, this situation develops out of what I have called the epic moment when the values and disciplines of American society stand balanced against the savage wilderness. The situation must involve a hero who possesses some of the urges toward violence as well as the skills, heroism and personal honor ascribed to the wilderness way of life, and it must place this hero in a position where he becomes involved with or committed to the agents and values of civilization. The nature of this situation, and of the conflict between town and wilderness which lies behind it imply that the formulaic pattern of action is that of chase and pursuit because it is in this pattern that the clash of savages and townspeople manifests itself. The savages attack the town and are pursued by the pioneers. Some of the pioneers leave the town and are pursued by the savages. The savages capture one or more of the townspeople and are pursued by the hero. An infinite number of variations are possible within the pattern of capture, flight and pursuit and the great majority of Westerns are structured around one or more of these types of action. Perhaps the most typical of all such patterns is that of the alternating flight and pursuit. The outlaws or Indians attack the town and are pursued by the hero and the pioneers; something happens to reverse the situation, an ambush or a mistaken splitting of forces, and the pursuers become the pursued. Finally, the hero succeeds in isolating the true villain from the group of savages and the situation reverses a third time, the hero's pursuit leading to the final confrontation which resolves the story. This built-in structural emphasis on the chase is of course one major reason why the Western has proved so adaptable to film and television presentation. Within these broad outlines the Western has been capable of absorbing many different plots from many different kinds of literature while retaining the flavor of a Western. Or to put it another way, so long as a story can be adapted to Western settings and characters and somehow reduced to the terms of flight, capture and pursuit almost anything can be reduced to a Western. Television Westerns in particular have adapted plots from every conceivable source; I recall one episode of *Bonanza* where the plot was clearly derived from a combination of Mary Shelley's *Frankenstein* and John Steinbeck's *Of Mice and Men* manipulated in such a way as to manifest a large proportion of pursuit. Such far-fetched adaptations are generally inferior to Westerns which develop plots which more directly articulate the implicit conflicts of the setting and character roles, but the possible range of Western plots is nonetheless quite wide.

VI

These, then, are the chief characteristics of the Western formula: a particular kind of setting, type of situation, and cast of characters with a strong emphasis on a certain kind of hero. I have indicated several ways in which this combination of elements possesses great dramatic power and unity. In the hands of skillful writers and directors who understand these relationships and know how to exploit them, Westerns can become highly effective works of art. Their actions are capable of arousing strong feelings, their quality of spectacle gives an epic sense to these actions and their structures are simple and clear enough to be widely understood and appreciated, even by children. This artistic power of unity of character, setting and action is surely the major source of the Western's long-term popularity as a formula.

However, though the intrinsic dramatic vigor and unity of the Western formula plays the major role in its success, this is not the whole story of the Western's popularity. For we must still ask why a particular artistic form or structure of conventions possesses dramatic power for the audiences who enjoy it, and what sort of dramatic power this is. There seem to be two levels on which this question can be answered. First, we can refer a particular form to some universal conception of types or genres, based presumably on innate qualities or characteristics of the human psyche. According to this approach, which has been followed by various literary theorists from Aristotle to Northrop Frye, a particular work or group of works becomes successful insofar as it effectively carries out an archetypal structure, which is in turn based on either innate human capacities and needs or on fundamental and universal patterns of experience. Using such a universal system as that suggested in Northrop Frye's *Anatomy of Criticism*, it is fairly simple to outline the relationship between the Western and archetypal forms. The Western is a fine example of what Frye calls the *mythos* of romance, a narrative and dramatic structure which he characterizes as one of the four central myths or story forms in literature, the other three being comedy, tragedy and irony. As Frye defines it, "the essential element of plot in romance is adventure," and the major adventure which gives form to the romance is the quest. Thus, "the complete form of the romance is clearly the successful quest, and such a completed form has three main stages: the stage of the perilous journey and the preliminary minor adventures; the crucial struggle, usually some kind of battle in which either the hero or his foe, or both, must die; and the exaltation of the hero."[25] These characteristics certainly fit the Western. The central action of chase and pursuit dramatizes the quest, the climactic shoot-down embodies the crucial battle, and the movement of the hero from alienation to commitment is an example of the "recognition of the hero, who has clearly proved himself to be a hero even if he does not survive the conflict."

Other characteristics of romance, as Frye defines them, are also clearly present in the Western. The struggle between hero and villain; the tendency to present both figures as coming not from the town but from the surrounding landscape; the way in which the hero's action is commonly associated with the establishment of law and order. These qualities also relate the Western to romances of many different cultures and periods:

The central form of romance is dialectical: everything is focussed on a conflict between the hero and his enemy, and all the reader's values are bound up with the hero. Hence the hero of romance is analogous to the mythical Messiah or deliverer who comes from an upper world, and his enemy is analogous to the demonic powers of a lower world. The conflict however takes place in, or at any rate primarily concerns, our world in the middle.[26]

Even smaller details of the basic pattern of romance discussed by Frye find their echo in the Western. For example, there is the contrast between schoolmarm and dance-hall girl—"a polarization may thus be set up between the lady of duty and the lady of pleasure"—the central role of the horse—"the dragon [has] his opposite in the friendly or helping animals that are so conspicuous in romance, among which the horse

who gets the hero to his quest has naturally a central place"—
and there is the noble Indian, the natural man who lends some
of his power to the hero—"the characters who elude the moral
antithesis of heroism and villainy generally are or suggest
spirits of nature. They represent partly the moral neutrality of
the intermediate world of nature and partly a world of mystery
which is glimpsed but never seen, and which retreats when
approached .... Such characters are, more or less, children of
nature who can be brought to serve the hero."[27]

Many Western writers have been fully aware of the
relationship between the cowboy and the traditional figures of
romance. Owen Wister, who created his influential Virginian
at least partly in the model of the chivalric knight of the middle
ages, explicitly expressed this relationship in his essay on
"The Evolution of the Cow-Puncher":

No doubt Sir Launcelot bore himself with a grace and breeding of
which our unpolished fellow of the cattle trail has only the latent
possibility; but in personal daring and in skill as to the horse, the
knight and the cowboy are nothing but the same Saxon of different
environments, the polished man in London and the man unpolished
in Texas; and no hoof in Sir Thomas Mallory shakes the crumbling
plains with quadruped sounds more valiant than the galloping that
has echoed from the Rio Grande to the Big Horn Mountains.[28]

However, though we are undoubtedly correct in ascribing some
of the shape and effectiveness of the Western to the fact that it
is a contemporary embodiment of a literary pattern which has
demonstrated nearly universal human appeal by its
appearance in most cultures, we are still faced with the
problem of the particular cultural formula which has evolved
as the major specific example of this universal narrative and
dramatic pattern. In addition to the formula's built-in artistic
unity and its relation to archetypal patterns, we must also
examine its primary cultural dimensions of game, ritual and
collective dream.

Romance, as Frye's many examples indicate, comes at all
levels of complexity and sophistication. There are romances as

elaborate and arcane as Spenser's *Fairie Queen* and as simple as the comic strip adventures of Superman and Batman. These differences in complexity and sophistication reflect the cultural area in which the romance functions. The romances of a leisured aristocratic class with elaborately developed manners and a number of conscious cultural ideals are usually more elaborate than the folk-tales which have grown out of homogeneous village culture with less complex, less self-conscious cultural ideals. The conditions of successful mass romances are somewhat different from both aristocratic and folk romance. In heterogeneous modern societies, widely successful romances must be so constructed as to be accessible to diverse groups with rather divergent interests and values. Consequently they tend to resemble games in the clarity of their rules and patterns of action. As I have indicated earlier this game-like aspect of the formula permits anyone who knows the "rules"—and in our culture children are instructed in the rules of the Western from a very early age—to enjoy and appreciate the fine points of play, as well as to experience the sense of ego-enhancement that comes when "our side" wins.

Part of the Western's wide popularity then is due to the fact that it is a brilliantly articulated game whose formula structure has evolved narrative counterparts to the primary characteristics of a game structure: 1) a game must have clearly opposing players—usually in the large spectator sports, two sides. These form basic moral reference points to which the viewer or participant relates with clearly positive or negative feelings. Similarly in most clearly differentiated popular formulas we have sides: a hero or group of good people—the home team—and a villain or band of evildoers—the visitors. The relations between these sides dominate the action. 2) A game has a set of rules indicating which actions are legitimate and which are not; only certain moves can take place and they must happen in a certain order and move toward a particular result. Analogously, a formula story has a particular pattern of expectations. Certain situations occur and others are definitely excluded by the rules. 3) Finally, a game takes place on a certain kind of board or field whose shape and markings indicate the significance of particular actions. The formula story also depends on a particular kind of setting: an abstracted social structure and landscape which give meaning to particular actions. In this way, the Western hero's relation to the town is analogous to the football player's relation to the line of scrimmage.

Let us now see how these three charactristics are built into the Western formula. First, since a game is basically determined by its board or field, so a popular formula tends to be initially characterized by its setting. Thus, the secret-agent story and the Western differ in that one takes place in a setting dominated by the struggle of rival nations and is usually set in a contemporaneous time, while the other unravels itself on a field of action where the fifty yard line is the frontier and the major points of social and geographical topography are an advancing civilization on one side and a savage wilderness on the other. Against this background, a three-sided game is played out. There is the group of townspeople who stand for the whole complex of values associated with civilization; there are the villains who are characterized by their rejection or perversion of these values and by their closeness to the savagery and lawlessness of the surrounding wilderness; and finally, there is the hero whose part is basically that of the man in the middle. Unlike the townspeople the hero possesses or comes to possess the savage skills of violence and the lawless individualism of the villain group, but he is needed by and finally acts on the side of the group of townspeople. The pattern of expectations which characterizes the Western is too complex to spell out in any detail here, but some of its main lines can be indicated. There must be a series of acts of violence to set the three-sided game in operation and to provoke and justify final destruction of the villain in such a way as to benefit the good group. Usually these acts are worked out in a sequence of chase and pursuit which can make use of the Western field of action and its particular form of movement, the horse, to the greatest extent. The goal of the game is to resolve the conflict between the hero's alienation and his commitment to the good group of townspeople. Thus, Westerns can end in many different ways. Sometimes the hero gets killed; sometimes he rides off into the desert; sometimes he marries the rancher's daughter and becomes a leading citizen. As I have alaready noted, important differences in cultural attitude are indicated by changes in the kinds of resolution which are the most common ways of ending the "game" at different times. It is no doubt significant that the great majority of Westerns in the first three decades of the twentieth century follow Wister's *The Virginian* in creating plots of romantic synthesis. The typical Zane Grey story or pulp Western of the 20s and 30s associated the hero's victory over the villain with his assimilation into the developing society. Usually, he married the school teacher or the rancher's daughter. After World War II however, the most significant Westerns have dealt with the gunfighter. In the typical gunfighter story the hero's violence, though necessary to the defeat of evil, nonetheless disqualifies him for the civilized society which he is saving. Similarly, in this more recent type of Western, the group of townspeople is usually presented in a far more ambiguous way, as if there were some question whether they merited the hero's sacrifice.

The social implications of these changing resolutions to the Western "game" indicate another dimension of the formula. I suggested earlier that popular formulas can be partly understood as social rituals. The structure of the Western bears this out. A ritual is a means of reaffirming certain basic cultural values, resolving tensions and establishing a sense of continuity between present and past. The Western, with its historical setting, its thematic emphasis on the establishment of law and order, and its resolution of the conflict between civilization and savagery on the frontier, is a kind of foundation ritual. It presents for our renewed contemplation that epic moment when the frontier passed from the old way of life into social and cultural forms directly connected with the present. By dramatizing this moment, and associating it with the hero's agency, the Western reaffirms the act of foundation. In this sense, the Western is like a Fourth of July ceremony. Moreover, while the Fourth of July ceremony has no room for dramatic conflict and ambiguity of values, the Western is able to explore not only what was gained, but what was lost in the movement of American history. In other words, the Western is effective as a social ritual because within its basic structure of resolution and reaffirmation, it indirectly confronts those uncertainties and conflicts of values which have always existed in American culture, but which have become increasingly strong in the twentieth century.

The dialectical structure of the Western—its opposition of townspeople and savages with the hero in the middle— encourages the expression of value oppositions. The same kind of plot patterns which made it possible for Cooper to explore his ambiguous feelings about civilization and nature, served Owen Wister's sense of a conflict between traditional and modern American. Still more recently, the Western dialectic has focussed on mid-twentieth century conflicts about the relation between law and order and private violence. Since Wister demonstrated so clearly that the nineteenth century Western formula could be resurrected from the dime novel, and made to embody contemporaneous adult attitudes and value conflicts, the Western has been important as a popular mode of exploring and resolving cultural tensions. We can still see this process in operation at the present day as Westerns explore some of the primary concerns of our own time such as racial conflict and collective violence. Generally, the Western's treatment of these issues is ritualistic rather than original. The almost wholly commercial circumstances of its creation, the fact that it is defined as entertainment, and the broad popular audience to which it appeals place a premium on the resolution of conflict and the affirmation of existing cultural values. Consequently, the Western rarely makes a truly profound or transcendent statement about the conflicts it expresses. Also, the highly conventionalized tradition of the Western does not encourage new interpretations of the American past. Nevertheless, within its limits, the Western formula does allow serious attempts on the part of creators and audience to relate contemporaneous conflicts to a vision of the American past. Perhaps for this reason, such traditional American rituals as the Fourth of July ceremony have increasingly declined into carnivals and fireworks displays, while the Western has continued to flourish.

Because the tradition of the Western has been continually renewed by extending its basic plot patterns to express shifting contemporaneous tensions, it is impossible to give anything like a full account of the Western as social ritual without examining in some detail the evolution of the Western formula. However, we can give some indication in a general way of the relation between the Western and American social values by exploring the Western formula's structural resolution of certain cultural ambiguities which have grown out of two major American ideals.

Progress is a prevailing ideal of collective social development in America and success has been a primary individual ideal. Both ideals emphasize change and improvement; they celebrate leaving behind the past and the status quo for a better, richer, happier future. In many ways, these two ideals have shaped the central political and social attitudes of most Americans. They have each given rise to a central hero figure and a myth which is celebrated over and over again in public rituals. The hero of progress is the pioneer who struggles against hardships to advance civilization. Initially, the heroic pioneer was the farmer who faced the dangers of nature and the Indian to bring civilization to the frontier. Somewhat later, the westerning farmer was joined by the industrial pioneer, the industrialist and inventor who struggled to bring the country to a new technological level. The success ideal produced its hero in the self-made man, the poor country boy or immigrant who rose to wealth and power in the burgeoning city.

However, though progress and success were central values, the experience of many Americans did not after all coincide with them. For every self-made man, there were at least two who never made the leap out of the lower or lower-middle classes, and there was a third who experienced a progressive decline in wealth and status. Nor did progress invariably appear as a collective improvement. In actuality every advance benefited some groups while it seriously harmed others. For example, the advance of the agricultural frontier benefited many, but it destroyed the Indians and ruined those engaged in the fur trade. The development of industry was progressive for much of the middle-class but a threat to the traditional landed gentry and to the small entrepreneur. Many technological advances were ambiguously mixed blessings. Every important new invention greatly improved some aspect of life but brought with it a whole range of new problems. In general, then, every individual success and every aspect of collective progress had its price. Some person or group had to pay the cost in economic loss, changed status or psychological readjustment to a new situation. However, the ideals of progress and success had no room for those who didn't make it. On the whole, Americans, at least in their public faith, refused to accept the fact that progress had its costs and success its ambiguities. Faith in the guiding hand of divine providence and confidence in the special historical mission of their country assured them that progress and success were benevolent processes. Thus, those individuals who paid the cost, instead of being offered sympathy and compassion, were stigmatized as failures. Groups who did not fit in with the general trend of social progress were forced to adjust or be eliminated. The destruction of the Indians symbolized in an extreme form the American way of treating obstacles to progress.

Though the public ideology had no meaningful consolation to offer those who suffered from progress, the experience of failure and obsolescence were common enough that substantial groups of Americans did not accept the ideals of success and progress without reservation. The most articulate of these groups consisted of writers, intellectuals and members of social elites whose traditional authority was threatened by social change. In the nineteenth century both serious writers and status-threatened aristocrats had reason to be aware of the ambiguities of success and progress for they were certainly not among its beneficiaries. Nineteenth century American novels often dealt with the cost of progress and the ambiguities of success. Cooper, both writer and member of a landed gentry which was losing the social authority it claimed as a right, created the first significant Western novels out of just such a thematic exploration of the cost of advancing civilization which he saw in terms of the destruction of the wilderness and the loss of "natural" society. In still more complex ways, Hawthorne and Melville explored the implications of the ideal of progress and warned in their rich and dark allegories that its price was even greater on the moral and psychological level. In *Pierre*, Melville tried to analyze some of the ambiguities of success, taking as his protagonist that archetypal success-hero, the young man from the country who comes to the city to make his way. But instead of fame and fortune, Melville's Pierre found horror and death. Later writers, Howells and his naturalistic followers in particular, explored the failure of success more fully, until Dreiser could portray the drive to succeed as the chief cause of the sordid and pathetic story of crime and punishment he called *An American Tragedy*.

Serious American literature, then, early became critical of the ideals of success and progress. For much of the nineteenth century, however, popular formula literature, those stories of adventure, domestic romance, sentiment and didacticism created by writers like T.S. Arthur, Mrs. Southworth and Horatio Alger, fully celebrated the dream of success and the glory of progress. In the later nineteenth century, however, popular adventure stories began to develop another kind of fictional pattern. This pattern initially appeared in the pulps and dime novels which dealt with the adventures of benevolent outlaws like Deadwood Dick or which romanticized the violence of actual western badmen like Billy the Kid, Jesse James and Wild Bill Hickock. Typically in these stories the outlaw was represented as a decent person who had been unjustly treated by the rich and powerful, or by women. Often these stories represented the benevolent outlaw's discovery, judgment and punishment of the respectable villains whose treachery had originally branded him an outlaw. There is doubtless some connection between this literature and the long-standing popular tradition of sensational literature dealing with criminals and rogues, a literature which probably also expressed a latent resentment and rebelliousness against the upper classes. However, the American glorification of the outlaw was significantly different from this tradition. The sensational literature of crime and roguery did not present the outlaw hero as a supremely moral man whose "crimes" were actually heroic acts of private justice. However much his skill and daring might be admired, the traditional rogue was an immoralist who rejected moral restraints whether they were man-made or decreed by God. Moreover in most instances the traditional rogue either reformed or came to a bad end. On the other hand, the benevolent outlaw, like the earlier mythical Robin Hood, not only proved to be the most honorable and moral character in the story, but he also usually defeated those who tried to use the cloak of respectability and legality to justify their evil acts. It was this pattern of the marginal hero exposing the corruption and decadence of the seemingly respectable members of society that eventually developed into the contemporary Western.

This pattern of popular literature reflected some doubts about the public ideals of success and progress, but rather than facing the ambiguities and failures of these ideals directly as did novelists like Cooper, Melville, Howells and Dreiser, the creators of popular adventure fiction worked out a pattern of action which resolved in fantasy the conflict between the ideals of success and progress and the actual pressures and tensions of American life. By creating a marginal hero whose style of behavior and mode of life identified him with those individuals and groups who, like the cowboy, belonged to a class that was rapidly becoming obsolete through social progress, these writers created a hero whose predicament reflected the ambiguities of these ideals. However, instead of exploring the cost of success and progress by representing their destructive impact on this hero, the creators of Westerns made their heroes into men of honor, physical strength and skill who were fully capable of withstanding the pressures and frustrations of their marginal social positions. Despite the pressure of temptation and threat, these heroes created and lived by an individual standard of justice and honor. With such a hero, the creators of Westerns were able to express some sense of ambiguity about these ideals and yet at the same time to reaffirm the essential benevolence of American progress. For, while the hero rejected many of the values of the pioneer and the self-made man, and had the courage and strength to act in accordance with his personal code, it was always the pioneer and the self-made man who ultimately prevailed. Either the hero joined them and became himself a success, as in Wister, or used his skill in violence to help found the pioneer community and then rode off into the desert, like Shane. Thus, from the point of view of social ritual, the meaning of the Western formula's point of plot and character is that of offering the hero a choice between civilization with its ideals of progress and success and anarchistic savagery with its spontaneity and freedom. The ritual is accomplished when we see that the hero, despite his own inability to live under these ideals and despite the corruption and falsity which these ideals often produce in such figures as the banker-villain, nonetheless chooses to act in such a way as to further the social order based on these ideals. Like many figures in American literature, the Western hero is something of an anti-hero to the self-made man and embodies strong feelings of hostility to the symbols and values of progress and success. Nonetheless his ritual role is one of resolving this hostility by concentrating it upon particular villains.

Though the Western remains officially on the side of progress and success, shifting formula patterns in the twentieth century reflect an increasing disillusion with these labels. In Wister, Zane Grey, Harold Bell Wright and many of the pulps of the twenties and thirties, the hero is a cowhand who, after proving his honor and independence, marries the schoolmarm or the rancher's daughter and settles down to become a self-made man. Thus, these Westerns still express the sense that there is a real synthesis possible between social progress, success and the heroic virtues of individual honor and masculine independence. However, as we approach the present, the ritualistic affirmation of progress and success becomes more and more ambiguous and strained. In gunfighter Westerns like Jack Schaefer's *Shane*, the hero destroys the villains, but at the cost of his own relation to the new society. The heroic marshal finds himself increasingly at odds with the pioneering townspeople whose avarice, selfishness and cowardice play a central thematic role in many contemporary Westerns. Two of the most successful Westerns of 1969, *The Wild Bunch* and *Butch Cassidy and the Sundance Kid*, actually went so far as to reverse the usual pattern of the formula Western and to present the unregenerate, lawless outlaw as a sympathetic figure by expressing a definite sense of regret at his elimination by the agents of law and. order. Though the Western has made a speciality of sympathetic outlaws throughout its history, the outlaw-heroes of these two films have fewer of the conventional marks of nobility and virtue than ever before. They are professional criminals rather than men driven to a life of crime by some wrong done them. Yet since they represent a more spontaneous, individualistic and free way of life, their destruction by the brutal, massive and corrupt agencies of the state is presented critically. Thus, it seems that we have come to a point where it is increasingly difficult to imagine a synthesis between the honor and independence of the Western hero and the imperatives of progress and success. In such a pattern, the ritual action reaffirms the inevitability of progress but suggests increasing disillusion and uncertainty about its consequences.

Yet though it is particularly central in recent Westerns, this theme of essential discrepancy between the demands of society and the heroic individual's honor and freedom has always been near the surface of the Western. It is even implicit in the original legend of Daniel Boone which inspired Cooper to create his Leatherstocking: Boone, the man who guided the settlers into the dark and bloody ground of Kentucky, who appears at the head of the column of men, women and children bringing civilization to the wilderness in Caleb Bingham's famous painting, was the ultimate pioneer; yet Boone, the man who had to move further West because the other settlers kept getting too close, was the original subversive and exile from civilization. Put the two together and we have the Lone Ranger, a hero who fights to bring law and order to the West yet who continually flees the very communities he has helped to found. This seemingly paradoxical aspect of the Western, this material which contradicts the surface message of affirmation of the advance of civilization, can be considered in two ways. First, as social ritual these conflicting themes can be understood as the operation of the dialectic of resolution which we have defined as the essential ritual structure of the Western. By presenting the conflict between key American values like progress and success and the lost virtues of individual honor, heroism and natural freedom and then resolving this conflict by showing the hero as a central agent in the foundation of society, the Western affirms the necessity of society and either demonstrates the social relevance of heroic virtue or justifies its loss by the benefits of social order and progress.

Second, despite this ritual affirmation of the central values of American society, a tension remains which is never quite fully resolved, particularly in the most powerful and artistically significant Westerns. Sometimes this tension shows itself in a definite sense of loss; when Leatherstocking heads for the wilderness again, we cannot help but feel that for all of Cooper's assurances there is something lacking in the new social order. The same thing is true of Shane's disappearance, or the decline of Tom Doniphon in Ford's *The Man Who Shot Liberty Valance*. In other instances, like *The Virginian*, the resolution, though happy, is touched with a sense of artificiality and fantasy, as if it were a little too good to be true. These qualities of feeling, which it is difficult to define precisely, reflect, I believe, that aspect of popular formulas which I defined earlier as collective dreaming.

At this point it becomes necessary for me to differentiate my conception of the social and psychological implications of popular formulas from the functional interpretations which I criticized earlier in this essay. The functionalist assumption— as carried through in such an essay as Dr. Munden's psychoanalytic interpretation of the Western—is that social or psychological dynamics directly cause the characters and action of literary works which, as a consequence, cannot be truly and deeply interpreted in any other way than by reference to their symbolic expression of certain social or psychic complexes. On the contrary, I have argued that works of art, whether popular or elite, highbrow or lowbrow, are autonomous realms of experience which are governed first by their own laws and secondarily and indirectly by social or psychological dynamics. Moreover I have suggested that we cannot interpret works of art in terms of a single dynamic, but that insofar as we seek to relate the artistic realm to culture we must see it as the intersection and interplay of several factors.

With these reservations in mind, I think we can safely assert one important difference between popular formulas and unique works of art with respect to their psychological dimension. All works of art presumably have latent psychological implications, but insofar as the creator moves away from purely conventional structures toward unique form, he is moving in the direction of conscious expression and exploration of latent meanings. Conventionalized formulas, however, tend to disguise and conceal these latent meanings because, to carry out their primary function as sources of artistic pleasure for a wide popular audience, they must not make people overtly aware of motives or conflicts that endanger their conventional view of themselves and their culture. The disguise of psychic conflict is not the primary cause of popular formulas but may be an important condition of their success.

As I suggested earlier, the problem of latent meanings can be investigated on two levels, the universal and the cultural. Psychoanalysts who have discussed literature seem to agree with Dr. Munden that, in one form or another, the universal latent meaning of most stories derives from the oedipal conflict. Insofar as we are interested in whatever latent meaning the Western has in common with all other stories and myths, some such conclusion seems justified. Here, however, we are not primarily concerned with this universal level of meaning which we can happily leave to the theories of the mythical and archetypal critics. Instead we are interested in latent feelings characteristic of American culture which might help account for the unique character of the Western formula. Since we have already noted the special connection between the Western formula and adolescent readers and movie-goers, this is probably the best place to begin a discussion of the ticklish subject of the Western as dream. If we accept Freud's conception of the dream as an expression in symbolism of unresolved conflicts between latent impulses and the attitudes of the conscious self, we can at least suggest a tentative interpretation of the Western from the perspective of its relevance to the cultural situation of adolescents. From this point of view, I suggest that the Western expresses the conflict between the adolescent's desire to be an adult and his fear and hesitation about the nature of adulthood. Let me support this contention by considering some of the central elements of the Lone Ranger, which is a supreme example of the kind of Western specifically created for and extremely successful with children. First,the hero is a masked man who conceals his true identity and constantly turns up in disguises, almost invariably as bearded older figures such as an old prospector. This kind of hero and this sort of behavior express a fascination with the problem of social roles and an attempt to create a person who can put roles on and off like disguises. Moreover the fact that the Lone Ranger not only moves in and out of disguises but also in and out of society might be interpreted as another symbolic expression of the conflict between a fascination with the adult world and a real hesitation to become committed to it. We might consider the relationship with Tonto in the same light, particularly if we recall, with the help of Leslie Fiedler's famous discussion of this subject, how much the theme of a young man's association with an older Indian or black man has been a part of a classic literature of adolescent initiation in our culture, from Cooper's *Deerslayer* through *Huckleberry Finn* to Faulkner's "The Bear."

Second, if we consider the kind of action which typically serves as the basis of Lone Ranger plots, we see that it, too, hints at ambiguous feelings about adulthood. The Lone Ranger typically exposes and brings to justice those figures who exemplify the corruption of adult power: the greedy and treacherous banker who seeks to cheat the farmers out of their rightful earnings; the tyrannical rancher who seeks to drive out the humbler settlers; the powerful outlaw who seeks to take over the town and rob it. As Dr. Munden suggests in his essay, such events have obvious oedipal implications. The villain is the feared and hated father-figure while the farmer symbolizes the non-threatening aspect of the father. By exposing the corrupt villain and restoring the farmer to his rightful position, the hero expresses the forbidden wish to murder the evil father on the one hand while protecting himself from guilt by supporting the good father on the other. Thus the action of the Lone Ranger expresses and to a certain extent resolves the adolescent's ambiguity about the adult world.

Finally, by his ability to expose and punish the evildoers and to reward the good people, the Lone Ranger uses the power and potency associated with adulthood, symbolized by his skill with guns. By doing so he earns the undying gratitude of the adult world for saving it from its corruptions. Note also that the invariable final scene of a Lone Ranger film or program shows the grateful sheriff or homesteader looking for the Lone Ranger to thank him, only to hear the cry of "Hi-ho Silver" as the hero rides into the mysterious distance. Is it stretching it too much to suggest that this scene evokes a childish wish to be free to spurn parental love as something no longer needed? In short, to be a Lone Ranger means to escape from the restrictiveness and helplessness of childhood without incurring any sense of guilt or adult responsibility.

The dream aspect of the Lone Ranger then is a fantasy of the perpetuation of moral innocence and freedom from guilt into an adult world of power and aggression, which probably reflects that American obsession with the innocence of childhood so often explored by our major writers. How many major American novels by writers like Hawthorne, Melville, Mark Twain, James, Hemingway and Faulkner have dealt with our culture's failure to provide meaningful patterns of initiation into the responsibilities and limitations of adulthood? How many youthful protagonists from Melville's Pierre, through Mark Twain's Huckleberry Finn to Salinger's Holden Caulfield have faced the tragic complexities of loss of innocence and knowledge of evil? The Long Ranger and other Western heroes disguise this fear of the complexities and corruptions of adult life by combining moral purity and separation from society, with adult power and potency. Through their legitimate violence, they express fear and hostility toward adults and the desire to punish them for their corruption which adolescents, at least until the current generation, have not found it easy to express directly.

But though this kind of psychological fantasy is probably one of the factors which shaped those Westerns which, like the Lone Ranger, dime novels and pulp stories, were primarily for younger audiences, how does this relate to adult interest in Westerns? Since we can see the same sort of pattern operating in a more subtle fashion in a number of adult Westerns and we know that many adults read or watch the type of Western exemplified by the Lone Ranger, it seems safe to conclude that the same psychological dynamic of hostility and fear of society mixed with an inability to recognize this aggressive anger for what it is can be, at least at times, a source of tension for adults as well. Particularly in a culture where social values are so confused and ambiguous about the relation between the individual and society, where some values place a great emphasis on conformity, the fantasy of the hero who reluctantly but nobly aids the cause of social order by acts of individual violence probably corresponds to a widespread fantasy of legitimated aggression.

Moreover, America in the twentieth century has had to confront a number of profound and disturbing ambiguities about violence which stem from conflicting historical traditions and realities. The popular nineteenth century vision of America as a redeemer nation, a new peace-loving Christian democracy, innocent of the hatred and violence of the past and with a mission to bring peace, prosperity and democracy to the world was a compelling cultural self-image. Yet the vision contrasted profoundly with the reality of an inordinately high level of individual and social aggression, beginning with the revolution which created the new nation and continuing through domestic and foreign wars of moralistic conquest and the violent subjugation of black people and Indians. To preserve the self-image it has been necessary to disguise the aggressive impulses in these historical realities under the mask of moral purity and social redemption through violence. Thus there has always been an observable similarity between the pattern of justifying rhetoric used to defend American military policy and the Western drama. Indeed, one of our basic nineteenth century military goals, the expropriation of the Indian, served as one of the historical models for the Western.

From this point of view, we can see how the cultural need for a fictional pattern which would disguise the hero's aggressive impulses while yet permitting them a full and legitimated indulgence has shaped certain aspects of the Western formula, in particular the way in which it works toward a moral and stylistic differentiation of the hero's violence, which is legitimate and good, from that of the outlaws or savages which is lawless and evil. Many elements contribute to this differentiation: the hero's initial reluctance; his dislike of violence for its own sake; the way the villain increasingly forces violence upon him; the controlled, graceful ritualistic style with which the hero typically dispatches the villain; the emphasis on the hero's strict code of honor and integrity in contrast to the villain's uncontrollable impulses.

However it would be entirely unfair to dismiss all Westerns as simple fantasies of legitimated violence. Though this pattern may be one basic ingredient of the formula, the serious creator of Westerns invariably struggles to bring the problem of individual and collective aggression to a level of conscious awareness and to explore it in a more profound and complex fashion. Thus, Robert Warshow is quite correct when he argues that the serious Western's major claim to a high level of artistic significance lies in the fact that "it offers a serious orientation to the problem of violence which can be found almost nowhere else in our culture."[29] While it is true that the commitment to romantic entertainment and to the figure of a transcendent hero have made it difficult to do so, the best Westerns have always managed to suggest a more complex recognition of the ambiguities of violence than the formulaic fantasy of legitimated moralistic aggression.

VII

In the preceding pages I have argued, in essence, that a popular formula like the Western cannot be understood as the effect of any single factor. However simple the formula may be, the artistic elements and the social and psychological implications it synthesizes are extremely complex. Consequently, it is quite incorrect to think that the key to the Western's popularity lies in any particular social or psychological dynamic. Instead, the Western's capacity to accommodate many different kinds of meaning—the archetypal pattern of heroic myth, the need for social ritual and for the disguised expression of latent motives and tensions—as well as its ability to respond to changing cultural themes and concerns—have made the formula successful as popular art and entertainment over many generations. No one of these factors is necessarily more basic than any other except perhaps the artistic. For no matter how many social and psychological functions a formula fulfills, it will probably never survive unless from time to time it attracts the interest of original and imaginative artists who are capable of revitalizing its conventions and stereotypes to express contemporaneous concerns. Thus, only by understanding how many factors have interacted in the complex process of the Western's evolution can we hope to understand the Western as a cultural phenomenon and as an artistic creation.

Notes

[1]Martin Nussbaum, "Sociological Symbolism in the 'Adult Western',"
Social Forces, vol. 39 (Oct. 1960), p. 26.

[2]Frederick Elkin, "The Psychological Appeal of the Hollywood Western,"
The Journal of Educational Sociology, vol. 24 (Oct. 1950), p. 74.

[3]David Brion Davis, "Ten-Gallon Hero" in Hennig Cohen (ed.) *The
American Experience* (Boston: Houghton Mifflin, 1968), pp. 256-7.

[4]Davis, p. 256.

[5]Kenneth J. Munden, M.D., "A Contribution to the Psychological
Understanding of the Cowboy and His Myth," *The American Imago*, vol. 15,
no. 2 (Summer 1958), pp. 103-147.

[6]F.E. Emery, "Psychological Effects of the Western Film: A Study in
Television Viewing," *Human Relations*, vol. 12, no. 3 (1959), p. 201.

[7]Emery, p. 202.

[8]Emery, p. 205.

[9]Sheldon Sacks, "The Psychological Implications of Generic
Distinctions," *Genre*, vol. 1, no. 2 (April 1968), p. 106.

[10]Emery, p. 204.

[11]Emery, p. 205.

[12]Peter Homans, "Puritanism Revisited: An Analysis of the Contemporary
Screen-Image Western," *Studies in Public Communication*, no. 3 (Summer
1961), pp. 73-84.

[13]Homans, p. 82.

[14]Homans, p. 74.

[15]Homans, p. 82.

[16]Cf. Northrop Frye's discussion of myth in *Anatomy of Criticism*
(Princeton: Princeton University Press, 1957).

[17]Jean Piaget as quoted in Larrabee and Meyersohn (eds.), *Mass Leisure*
(Glencoe, IL: The Free Press, 1958), p. 71.

[18]Henry Nash Smith, *Virgin Land* (New York: Vintage Books, n.d.), p. 135.

[19]However, some recent Westerns present a much more complex treatment
of the Indian, constituting a significant departure from the tradition of the
Western; cf.such novels as Lott's *Dance Back the Buffalo*, Henry's *From Where
the Sun Now Stands* and Berger's *Little Big-Man;* and such films as *Run of the
Arrow* and *A Man Called Horse.*

[20]Cf. the excellent account of the impact of the West on Roosevelt,
Remington and Wister in G. Edward White, *The Eastern Establishment and
the Western Experience* (New Haven: Yale University Press, 1968).

[21]Leslie Fiedler, *Love and Death in the American Novel* (New York: Stein
and Day, 1966), p. 211.

[22]Ernest Haycox, *Man in the Saddle* (New York: Dell Publishing Co., 1966),
p. 9.

[23]Robert Warshow, *The Immediate Experience* (Garden City, N.Y.:
Anchor, 1964), p. 94.

[24]Warshow, p. 96.

[25]Frey, p. 186.

[26]Frye, p. 186.

[27]Frye, pp. 196-97.

[28]Owen Wister, "The Evolution of the Cowpuncher," in *Red Men and
White*, vol. VI of *The Writings of Owen Wister* (New York: Macmillan, 1928), p.
xxvii.

[29]Warshow, p. 103.

A. The Western Novel: A Selected Guide

A complete bibliography of the Western novel would constitute a huge volume in itself and would be difficult to distinguish at several points from a bibliography of American literature. Indeed, a number of writers have suggested that American literature and culture have been so pervasively influenced by the Western experience that they cannot be understood at all without reference to the West as historical reality, legend and myth. Frederick Jackson Turner in his essays on the significance of the frontier in American history [cf G.R. Taylor, ed., *The Turner Thesis* (Heath and Co.) for a convenient paperback selection of some of Turner's major essays together with critical essays on the Turner Thesis] first fully articulated this view which has greatly influenced American literary and historical scholarship since his time. Two major studies growing out of this concern with the significance of the frontier in American culture are particularly important to the study of the Western. The first, Henry Nash Smith's *Virgin Land*, sees the West not so much as a reality as a pervasive myth influencing American thought and action. Smith's study sets the Western in the larger context of cultural myths and is an indispensable reading for the student of the Western. The second work, Edwin Fussell's *Frontier*, sets forth the thesis that the frontier served as a controlling symbol in the major works of American literature in the first half of the nineteenth century. In effect, Fussell suggests that not only Cooper but most of our major writers including Melville, Hawthorne and Thoreau should be considered as creators of Westerns. Two earlier studies along Turnerian lines are Lucy L. Hazard, *The Frontier in American Literature* and Ralph L. Rusk, *The Literature of the Middle Western Frontier*.

This bibliography concerns itself not with the overall impact of the West on American culture and literature but with the nineteenth century shaping and twentieth century practice of a certain kind of fiction which might loosely be described as

115

stories and novels of the romantic or legendary West, a type of fiction that has centered around the sort of literary and cultural formula defined and discussed in the preceding essay. It is this kind of fiction that is most directly related to the Western film, which is also treated in this bibliographical guide. This romantic or legendary West can be loosely distinguished from the realistic and the humorous or satirical treatment of Western material. For an excellent discussion and bibliography of the nineteenth century tradition of Western humor, the reader should consult Walter Blair, *Native American Humor*. Unfortunately there is no single work which deals with the realistic treatment of the West in American literature, partly because the distinction between the Western as formulaic romance and the Western novel as realistic historical treatment of its subject is not a perfectly clear one. Instead, we find a continuum which ranges from the purely legendary Western like The Lone Ranger to a harsh and realistic account of Western experience without any epic or romantic qualities like Hamlin Galand's *Main-Travelled Roads* (1891). In between these poles lie a number of major works which are largely true to historical reality, but which do concern themselves with the mythical or legendary aspects of the West, works like Stephen Crane's "The Blue Hotel" or Walter Van Tilburg Clark's *The Ox-Bow Incident*. These works must be included in any serious study of the Western along with the more formulaic and romantic creations of writers like Zane Grey and Ernest Haycox.

This still leaves us with an enormous literature which we will sample only sparingly mainly in an effort to indicate the most important works and types of works from both artistic and cultural points of view. Professor Richard Etulian is preparing what we trust will be a more definitive bibliography which can be consulted for fuller and more detailed checklists of Western writers.

1. Early Shapers of the West

James Fenimore Cooper created the Western and the **enormous nineteenth** century popularity of his Western novels provided both model and impetus for most of the early development of the Western. Cooper's most important Western work is of course the "Leatherstocking Tales." *The Pioneers* (1823), *The Last of the Mohicans* (1826), *The Prairie* (1827), *The Pathfinder* (1840), *The Deerslayer* (1841). Though Cooper wrote a number of other novels with a Western setting, including *The Wept of Wish-ton-Wish* (1829) and *Wyandotte* (1843) the absence of the Western hero Natty Bumppo from these latter novels makes them distinctly less successful and suggests the extent to which a particular kind of hero has been central to the Western as a literary and cultural form. A handy collection of criticism of the Leatherstocking Tales is Warren S. Walker, *Leatherstocking and the Critics*.

Though Cooper originated the Western as we know it, his work synthesized a number of existing literary forms, most importantly: the form of the English historical romance primarily created by Sir Walter Scott; the cultural tradition of the noble savage (cf. Hoxie N. Fairchild, *The Noble Savage* for a study of that tradition); a number of American works concerning the Indian (see below); and the actual historical figure of Daniel Boone, already somewhat mythicized in the supposed autobiographical narrative included in John Filson, *Discovery, Settlement, and Present State of Kentucke* (1784).

Scholars have established that Cooper's primary source of Indian history and customs was John Heckewelder's *Account of the History, Manners, and Customs of the Indian Nations, Who Once Inhabited Pennsylvania and the Neighboring States* (1819) and Paul Wallace in an essay on "Cooper's Indians," *New York History* XXXV (Oct. 1954), 423-446, has analyzed the impact of this book on Cooper's imagination. However, there were probably a number of other sources which influenced Cooper's vision of the Indians. As Leslie Fiedler has pointed out, the Indian has always played a vital role in the tradition of the Western. Thus it is worth noting that the earliest form of Western account was the Indian captivity narrative, the first of which, was *The Sovereignty and Goodness of God ... Being a Narrative of the Captivity and Restoration of Mrs. Mary Rowlandson* (1682). The captivity narrative continued to be an important form of Western literature throughout the eighteenth and nineteenth centuries. For discussion and bibliography of captivity narratives see the following:

Barbeau, Marion. "Indian Captivities," *Proceedings of the Amerian Philosophical Society*, vol. 94, 522-48.
Hallowell, Irving, "American Indians White and Black: The Phenomenon of Transculturation," *Current Anthropology*, vol. 4, 519-29
Pearce, Roy Harvey, "The Significance of the Captivity Narrative," *American Literature*, vol. 19, 1-20.

The student of the mythical Indian in the Western will also find it very illuminating to consult the following studies of the Indian and American culture:

Pearce, Roy Harvey, *The Savages of America*
Keiser, Albert, *The Indian in American Literature*

Finally, Wilcomb Washburn, *The Indian and the White Man* is a very useful anthology containing a number of important selections reflecting attitudes toward the Indian including selections from Heckewelder's book mentioned above, and from Rousseau's discussion of the noble savage.

Following Cooper, a number of other mid-nineteenth century novelists used the frontier setting for at least some of their novels. The closest of these to Cooper's example and hence to the modern Western is Robert Montgomery Bird's *Nick of the Woods* (1837) written at least partly in response to what its author believed to be Cooper's highly sentimentalized and fanciful, not to say dangerously misleading portrayal of the Indians. It was the first in a tradition of literary attacks on Cooper's version of the West which includes such minor gems as Mark Twain's "Literary Offenses of James Fenimore Cooper," Bret Harte's "Muck-a-Muck" and Thackeray's "The Stars and Stripes."

Other significant Western novels of the period:

French, James S., *Elkswatawa; or the Prophet of the West. A Tale of the Frontier* (1836).
Tucker, Nathaniel B., *George Balcombe* (1836).
Simms, William Gilmore, *The Yemassee* (1835), several of Simms's other novels such as *The Scout*(1841), *Woodcraft* (1854), *The Forayers* (1855), *Border Beagles* (1840), which involve frontier settings.
Paulding, James K., *Westward Ho!* (1832).

Hall, James, *Sketches of History, Life and Manners in the West* (1834), *Legends of the West* (1853).

Webber, Charles W., *Old Hicks, the Guide, Or, Adventures in the Camanche Country in Search of a Gold Mine* (1848).

It should also be noted that this was the period of the development of a very different kind of frontier figure, best illustrated in the public character and autobiographical narratives of Davy Crockett. The relationship between the Leatherstocking hero and the Crockett hero is examined in Jules Zanger, "The Frontiersman in Popular Fiction," in J.F. McDermott, ed., *The Frontier Re-examined."*

One other writer of great importance in presenting a vision of the West was Francis Parkman, the historian. His *Oregon Trail* (1849) was a classic account of a Western journey and his multi-volume history of the conflict of England and France in the New World has the kind of epic sweep and grandeur often attempted but rarely achieved by the writers of Western novels.

2. The Latter Half of the Nineteenth Century

During this period the Western evolves into a distinctive formula and diverges more sharply from the realistic novel of the West. With the shift of Western settlement to the Great Plains and the Far West, the cowboy emerges as the key heroic figure and the realistic novel of the West tends to turn away from the Wild West and the frontier to an examination of the harsh and narrow life of farmers and small town dwellers in the Great Plains. The Western becomes a staple of the dime novel and the pulp weekly and in the process becomes increasingly formulaic and stereotyped. Finally, the emergence of the Wild West Show as a great public spectacle gives a new kind of vitality to the Western theme and paves the way for the Western's translation to the screen.

I will make no attempt to give anything like a complete list of serious novels with a Western setting in this period. A few of the most important are:

Hamlin Garland, *Main-Travelled Roads* (1891)

Frank Norris, *The Octopus* (1901)

Edgar Watson Howe, *The Story of a Country Town* (1883)

Willa Cather, *O Pioneers!* (1913), *My Antonia* (1918)

Alongside this treatment of the agricultural West in fiction there emerges a more colorful and mythically oriented fictional treatment of the West, leading to the creation of the modern adult Western in the works of Owen Wister. Some of the central works in this development are:

Bret Harte, *The Luck of Roaring Camp and Other Sketches* (1870), *Mrs. Skagg's Husbands and Other Sketches* (1873)

Mark Twain, *Roughing It* (1872)

Hamlin Garland, *The Captain of the Gray-Horse Troop* (1902)

Stephen Crane, *The Open Boat and Other Tales of Adventure* (1898) and *The Monster and Other Stories* (1899). These collections include the two great Western stories "The Bride Comes to Yellow Sky" and "The Blue Hotel," which probably represent the highest level of concentrated artistry in the Western story.

But it is in the dime novel and the pulp weekly that the romantic Western flourished most widely in this period. Some of the books treating this development are:

Albert Johannsen, *The House of Beadle and Adams*, a definitive study of the largest dime novel publisher including a complete listing of their publications.

Charles Bragin, *Bibliography of Dime Novels 1860-1964*

Mary Noel, *Villains Galore*, a study of the Weekly Storypaper which was another major medium for the publication of Westerns in the later nineteenth century.

Quentin Reynolds, *The Fiction Factory*, a history of the large publishing firm of Street and Smith.

Edmund Pearson, *Dime Novels*.

Henry Nash Smith, *Virgin Land* contains an excellent discussion of the development of the Western hero in the dime novel.

A convenient paperback reprint of two important dime novels is Philip Durham, ed., *Seth Jones and Deadwood Dick on Deck*. Charles W. Bragin of Brooklyn N.Y. has made a great many dime novels available in facsimile reprints and most large libraries hold substantial collections, the largest being probably that of the New York Public Library.

The immense popularity of the Wild West Show played an important part in the making of the Western. For an excellent bibliography on this subject as well as a thorough scholarly study of the life of Buffalo Bill Cody, the major figure in the development of the Wild West Show see Don Russell, *The Lives and Legends of Buffalo Bill*.

In the later nineteenth century, legends rapidly evolved around many of the actual scouts, soldiers, cowboys and badmen of the West. As Daniel Boone had become a national hero in the early nineteenth century, so individuals like Kit Carson, General Custer, Wild Bill Hickok and Billy the Kid become mythical figures in the later nineteenth century. For a careful study of this process and a good bibliography of legendary books and stories about a number of these figures see Kent Ladd Steckmesser, *The Western Hero in History and Legend*. On the relationship between Western heroes and other American hero-types see Dixon Wecter, *The Hero in America*, and Marshall Fishwick, *The American Hero*.

3. The Early Twentieth Century

With the appearance of Owen Wister's *The Virginian* (1902) and Porter's film *The Great Train Robbery* (1903) the modern Western was born, synthesizing some of the adventurous and mythical qualities of the dime novels with more sophisticated and adult treatments of history, setting and character. Six writers stand out as particularly significant creators of Westerns in the first two decades of the twentieth century.

a. **Owen Wister.** Wister's *The Virginian* (1902) was a brilliant synthesis of the romantic and the realistic. In his cowboy hero, Wister combined aspects of the Leatherstocking tradition with the newer image of the heroic horseman of the Great Plains and created a figure and a type of story so successful that it can be called the basis of the modern Western. Wister's novel has sold over two million copies, has served as the basis of several movies and a successful television series. Wister wrote one other good Western novel, *Lin McLean* and a number of fine stories.

b. **Andy Adams'** *The Log of a Cowboy* (1903), a semi-fictionalized account of the author's participation in a cattle drive is one of the great Western classics and perhaps the closest thing to a realistic treatment of the cowboy's life. A number of other works follow more or less the same lines though less successfully.

c. **Eugene Manlove Rhodes.** Though even the most realistic of Western writers are basically romantics at heart, some like Adams and Rhodes achieve a strong sense of verisimilitude in their work rather like the best films of John Ford. Rhodes' major works are *Good Men and True* (1910), *West is West* (1917) and *The Proud Sheriff* (1935). A convenient recent collection is Frank Bearing (ed). *The Best Novels and Stories of Eugene Manlove Rhodes* (1949).

d. **Zane Grey.** When we come to Zane Grey we enter the realm of the super-romantic. Grey's purple extravagances are sometimes painful for modern readers, but as one of the most prolific, bestselling writers of all time, he is of great cultural if not literary interest.

A selected list of his works follows:

Betty Zane 1904
The Spirit of the Border 1905
The Heritage of the Desert Outing Publishers
Riders of the Purple Sage 1910 Harper & Bros.
Desert Gold 1913 Harper
The Man of the Forest 1929 Harper
The Mysterious Rider 1921 Harper
To The Last Man 1922 Harper
The Border Legion 1916 Harper
The U.P. Trail 1918 Harper
The Call of the Canyon 1924 Harper
The Thundering Herd 1925 Harper
Code of the West 1934 Harper
Western Union 1939 Harper
Twin Sombreros 1942 Harper
Majesty's Rancho 1942 Harper
Shadow on the Trail 1946 Harper

e. **Emerson Hough.** Another prolific creator of Western fiction, similar to Grey in his combinations of history, romance and landscape.

The Story of the Cowboy 1897 Appleton & Co.
The Girl at the Half-Way House 1900 Appleton
The Way to the West 1903 Bobbs-Merrill
The Law of the Land 1905 Bobbs-Merrill
The Way of a Man 1907 The Outing Publishing Co.
The Story of an Outlaw 1907 Outing Publishing Co.
The Sowing 1909 Vanderhoof-Gunn Company, Ltd. *5440 or Fight* 1909 Bobbs-Merrill
The Purchase Price 1911 Bobbs-Merrill
The Magnificent Adventure 1916 Appleton
The Man Next Door 1917 Appleton
The Broken Gate 1917 Appleton
The Way Out 1918 Appleton
The Sagebrusher 1919 Appleton
The Passing of the Frontier 1918 Yale University Press
The Covered Wagon 1922 Appleton
North of 36 1923 Appleton
Mother of Gold 1924 Appleton
The Ship of Souls 1925 Appleton

f. **Alfred Henry Lewis.** Creator of the fine "Wolfville" stories and a writer in the tradition of Bret Harte.

4. Pulps and Paperbacks

In the twentieth century the pulp magazine and the cheap paperback have been two of the major forms of literary Western and their number is legion. Some idea of the immensity of Western publications in this form can be seen in another section of this guide which presents a list of pulp Western magazines published in the heyday of that form. To get some idea of the nature of a pulp writing career, the student should consult Frank Gruber's *The Pulp Jungle,* a memoir of the writer's years as a creator of pulps. To represent this group of writers, I have selected four of the most successful.

Max Brand (Frederick Faust)

The Untamed 1918 G.P. Putnam's Sons
The Night Horseman 1920 Putnam
Trailin' 1920 Putnam
The Seventh Man 1921 Putnam
Dan Bary's Daughter 1924
Gun Tamer 1929 Dodd, Mead & Co.
Destry Rides Again 1930 Dodd, Mead
Valley Vultures 1932 Dodd, Mead
Twenty Notches 1932 Dodd, Mead
The Longhorn Feud 1933 Dodd, Mead
The Outlaw 1933 Dodd, Mead
Brothers on the Trail 1934 Dodd, Mead
Rancher's Revenge 1934 Dodd, Mead
The Haunted Riders 1935 Dodd, Mead
The Rustlers of Beacon Creek 1935 Dodd, Mead
South of the Rio Grande 1936 Dodd, Mead
The Iron Trail 1937 Dodd, Mead
The Trouble Trail 1937 Dodd, Mead
Dead or Alive 1938 Dodd, Mead
Singin' Guns 1938 Dodd, Mead
Gunman's Gold 1939 Dodd, Mead
The Dude 1949 Dodd, Mead

Ernest Haycox

Chaffee of Roaring Horse 1930 Doubleday, Doran & Co.
All Trails Cross 1931 Doubleday
Starlight Rider 1933 Doubleday
Smoky Pass 1934 Doubleday
Riders West 1934 Doubleday
Trail Smoke 1936 Doubleday
Deep West 1937 Doubleday
Trouble Shooter 1937 Doubleday
Man in the Saddle 1938 Little, Brown
Sundown Jim 1938 Little, Brown
Rim of the Desert 1941 Little, Brown
Trail Town 1941 Little, Brown
Alder Gulch 1942 Little, Brown

Bugles in the Afternoon 1944 Little, Brown
Canyon Passage 1945 Little, Brown
Rough Justice 1950 Little, Brown
By Rope and Lead 1951 Little, Brown
Murder on the Frontier 1953 Little, Brown
The Adventurers 1954 Little, Brown

Luke Short (Frederick Glidden)

Marauders' Moon 1937 Dell (pub. 1953)
The Branded Man 1938 Dell (pub. 1953)
Hard Money 1940 Doubleday
Ride the Man Down 1942 Doubleday
Ramrod 1943 Macmillan
Coroner Creek 1946 Macmillan
Station West 1947 Houghton Mifflin
Fiddlefoot 1949 Houghton Mifflin
Vengeance Valley 1950 Houghton Mifflin
Play a Lone Hand 1950 Houghton Mifflin
Barren Land Murders 1950 Fawcett
Saddle by Starlight 1952 Houghton Mifflin
Silver Rock 1953 Houghton Mifflin
Bought With a Gun 1955 Dell
Rimrock 1955 Random House

Frank Gruber

Peace Marshal 1939 W. Morrow & Co.
Outlaw 1941 Farrar & Rinehart
Gunsight 1942 Dodd, Mead & Co.
Fighting Man 1948 Rinehart
Broken Lance 1949 Rinehart
Smoky Road 1949 Rinehart
Fort Starvation 1953
Quantrell's Raiders 1953 Ace Books
Better Sage 1954 Rinehart
Johnny Vengeance 1954 Rinehart
Bugles West 1954 Rinehart
The Highwayman 1955 Rinehart
Buffalo Brass 1956 Rinehart
Lonesome River 1957 Rinehart

Town Tamer 1958 Rinehart
The Marshal 1958 Rinehart
The Bushwackers 1959 Rinehart
Tales of Wells Fargo 1958 Bantam Books

5. The Contemporary Western Novel

There are many different varieties and levels of Western writing at the present time. The pulp-paperback tradition continues unabated in the works of writers like Will Henry (Henry W. Allen), Todhunter Ballard, Louis L'Amour, Iwe Hoffman, Donald Hamilton, Lewis Patten and a regiment of others. There is even an organization, the Western Writers of America, dedicated to sharing trade secrets and interests. The group publishes a regular magazine called *Roundup*; popular histories and historical novels of the West continue to come out at a tremendous rate and lavish publications like the *American Heritage History of the Great West* and the *American Heritage Book of the Pioneer Spirit* testify to the continuing fascination of the legend of the West. In literary terms, perhaps the most interesting development of recent years has been the emergence in both literature and film of a number of works which retain many of the traditional subjects and even formal characteristics of the Western such as an emphasis on action and a considerable simplicity of style but which engage in a more self-conscious, complex and critical examination of the legend of the West, and the literary and cinematic legends which have been built around it. Another sign of change in the Western is the emergence of much richer, more sympathetic and even admiring portrayals of the Indian. Such films as *The Wild Bunch, The Stalking Moon, A Man Called Horse, Butch Cassidy and the Sundance Kid* reflect the more complex attitudes found in such relatively recent novels as:

Allan Bosworth, *New Country*
Milton Lott, *Dance Back the Buffalo*
Thomas Berger, *Little Big Man* (cf. the film by Arthur Penn)
Larry McMurtry, *Leaving Cheyenne*
Frederick Manfred, *Lord Grizzly*
A.B. Guthrie, *The Way West* and *These Thousand*

Hills
Alan LeMay *The Searchers* (cf. the film by John
Ford)
Jack Schaefer, *Shane*
Walter Van Tilburg Clark, *The Ox-Box Incident*
Conrad Richter, *The Sea of Grass* and *The Light in
the Forest*

A number of these works are interestingly discussed in
Leslie Fiedler *The Return of the Vanishing American*. A more
literary discussion of a number of these writers can be found in
James C. Folsom, *The American Western Novel*. The most
useful journal for keeping track of the contemporary Western
novel is the interesting *Western American Literature* edited by
J. Golden Taylor. This journal publishes scholarly and critical
articles and contains an annual bibliography of studies in
Western American literature with listings by author.

B. Major Western Directors: Filmographies (compiled by Barbara Bernstein)

JOHN FORD (from Bogdanovitch, *John Ford*)

The Tornado 1917
The Scrapper 1917
The Soul Herder 1917
Cheyenne's Pal 1917
Straight Shooting 1917
A Secret Man 1917
A Marked Man 1917
Bucking Broadway 1917
The Phantom Riders 1918
Wild Women 1918
Thieves' Gold 1918
The Scarlet Drop 1918
Hell Bent 1918
A Woman's Fool 1918
Roped 1919
The Fighting Brothers 1919
A Fight for Love 1919
By Indian Post 1919
The Rustlers 1919

Bare Fists 1919
Gun Law 1919
The Gun Packer 1919
Riders of Vengeance 1919
The Last Outcast 1919
The Outcasts of Poker Flat 1919
The Rider of the Law 1919
Marked Men 1919
The Freeze Out 1919
The Wallop 1921
Desperate Trails 1921
Action 1921
Three Jumps Ahead 1923
North of Hudson Bay 1923
The Iron Horse 1924
Lightnin' 1924
Three Bad Men 1926
Stagecoach 1939
Drums Along the Mohawk 1939
My Darling Clementine 1946
Three Godfathers 1948
Fort Apache 1948
She Wore a Yellow Ribbon 1949
Wagon Master 1950
Rio Grande 1950
The Searchers 1956
Sergeant Rutledge 1960
Two Rode Together 1961
The Man Who Shot Liberty Valance 1962
How The West Was Won (Civil War Episode) 1962
Cheyenne Autumn 1964

WILLIAM S. HART (from Eyles, *The Western*)
Directed by Hart

The Passing of Two-Gun Hicks
My Silent Haskind
The Scourge of the Desert
The Sheriff's Streak of Yellow
The Taking of Luke McVane

The Darkening Trail 1915
The Ruse 1915
Cash Parrish's Pal
The Conversion of Frosty Blake 1918
Grit
Keno Bates, Liar
The Disciple
The Aryan 1916
Hell's Hinges 1916
The Primal Lure 1916
The Desert Man 1916
Pinto Ben 1916
The Return of Draw Egan 1916
The Devil's Double 1916
The Silent Man 1917
The Cold Deck 1917
The Gunfighter 1917
The Square Deal Man 1917
Truthful Gulliver 1917
Wolf Lowry 1917

Directed by Lambert Hillyer

The Narrow Trail 1917
Blue Blazes Rawden 1918
Border Wireless 1918
Branding Broadway 1918
Riddle Game 1918
Selfish Yates 1918
Shark Monroe 1918
The Tiger Man 1918
Wolves of the Rail 1918
Breed of Men 1919
John Petticoats 1919
The Money Corral 1919
Square Deal Sanderson 1919
Wagon Tracks 1919
Sand 1919
The Roll Gate 1920
O'Malley of the Mounted 1920

White Oak 1921
Tree Word Band 1921
Travelin' On 1921

The Testing Black 1929

Directed by Cliff Smith

Wild Bill Hickock
Singer Jim McKee

Directed by King Baggott

Tumbleweeds

ANTHONY MANN (From Kitses, *Horizons West*)

The Devil's Doorway 1950
The Furies 1950
Winchester 73 1950
Bend of the River 1952
The Naked Spur 1953
The Far Country 1955
The Man From Laramie 1955
The Last Frontier 1956
The Tin Star 1957
Man of the West 1958
Cimarron 1960

HOWARD HAWKS

Red River 1948
The Big Sky 1952
Rio Bravo 1959
El Dorado 1967
Rio Lobo 1970

SAM PECKINPAH (From Kitses)

The Deadly Companion 1962
Ride The High Country 1962

Major Dundee 1965
The Wild Bunch 1968
The Ballad of Cable Hogue 1970

BUDD BOETTICHER (From Kitses)

The Cimarron Kid 1951
Bronco Buster 1952
Horizons West 1952
Seminole 1953
The Man From The Alamo 1953
Wings of the Hawk 1953
Seven Men From Now 1956
The Tall T 1957
Decision at Sundown 1957
Buchanan Rides Alone 1958
Ride Lonesome 1959
Westbound 1959
Comanche Station 1960
A Time for Dying 1969

SAMUEL FULLER

I Shot Jesse James 1949
The Baron of Arizona 1950
Run of the Arrow 1957
Forty Guns 1957
Merrill's Marauders 1962
Shark (Twist of the Knife) shot 1968-9 Unreleased

HENRY HATHAWAY (From Eyles, *The Western)*

Wild Horse Mesa 1933
Heritage of the Desert 1933
Under the Tonto Rim 1933
Sunset Pass 1933
Man of the Forest 1933
To The Last Man 1933
Last Round Up 1934
Thundering Herd 1934

Trail of the Lonesome Pine 1936
Go West, Young Man 1936
Brigham Young 1938
Rawhide 1951
From Hell to Texas 1958
North to Alaska 1960
How The West Was Won 1963
The Sons of Katie Elder 1965
Nevada Smith 1966
True Grit 1969

WILLIAM WELLMAN

The Man Who Won 1923
The Vagabond Trail 1924
Not a Drum Was Heard 1924
The Circus Cowboy 1924
The Conquerers 1932
Stingaree 1934
Robin Hood of El Dorado 1935
The Great Man's Lady 1942
The Ox-Bow Incident 1943
Buffalo Bill 1944
Yellow Sky 1951
Across the Wide Missouri 1950
Westward The Women 1950
Track of the Cat 1954

MICHAEL CURTIZ (From Eyles)

Under A Texas Moon 1930
River's End 1931
Mountain Justine 1937
Gold is Where You Find It 1938
Dodge City 1939
Virginia City 1940
Santa Fe Trail 1940
Jim Thorpe, All American 1951
The Boy From Oklahoma 1954
The Proud Rebel 1958

The Hangman 1959
The Commancheros 1961

RAOUL WALSH (From Eyles)

The Life of Villa 1912
Betrayed 1917
The Conqueror 1917
In Old Arizona 1929
The Big Trail 1930
The Dark Command 1940
They Died With Their Boots On 1942
Pursued 1947
Cheyenne 1947
Silver City 1948
Colorado Territory 1949
Along The Great Divide 1951
Distant Drums 1951
The Lawless Breed 1951
Gun Fury 1953
Saskatchewan 1954
The Tall Men 1955
The King and Four Queens 1956
The Sheriff of Fractured Jaw 1958
A Distant Trumpet 1964

FRITZ LANG

The Return of Frank James 1940
Western Union 1941
Rancho Notorious 1952

ALLAN DAWN (From Eyles)

The Pretty Sister of Jose 1915
The Half-Breed 1916
The Good-Bad Man 1916
Frontier Marshal 1939
Trail of the Vigilantes 1940
Montana Belle 1952

The Woman They Almost Lynched 1953
The Silver Lode 1954
Passion 1954
Cattle Queen of Montana 1954
Tennessee's Partner 1955
The Restless Breed 1957

ARTHUR PENN

The Left-Handed Gun 1958
The Chase 1966
Little Big Man 1970

KING VIDOR

Billy The Kid 1930
The Texas Rangers 1936
Duel in the Sun 1944
Man Without A Star 1955

NICHOLAS RAY

The Lusty Men 1952
Johnny Guitar 1954
Run for Cover 1955
The True Story of Jesse James 1957
Wind Across The Everglades 1958

RICHARD BROOKS

The Last Hunt 1955
The Professionals 1966

MARLON BRANDO

One-Eyed Jacks 1961

GEORGE ROY HILL

Butch Cassidy and the Sundance Kid 1969

SYDNEY POLLACK

Scalphunters 1968

DON SIEGEL

Battle at Silver Creek 1953
Flaming Star 1960
Two Mules for Sister Sara 1970

C.A. Chronological List of Major & Representative Westerns

1903	*The Great Train Robbery* Edwin S. Porter
1909	*Boots and Saddles*
1911	*Fighting Blood* D.W. Griffith
1913	*Bronco Billy's Oath*
1913	*The Heart of an Indian* Thomas Ince
1913	*The Squaw Man* Cecil B. DeMille
1915	*The Spoilers* Colin Campbell
1916	*Hell's Hinges* William S. Hart
1916	*Manhattan Madness* (Douglas Fairbanks) Allan Dwan
1917	*The Aryan* William S. Hart
1919	*The Outcasts of Poker Flat* John Ford
1920	*The Last of the Mohicans* Maurice Tourneur
1923	*Covered Wagon* James Cruze
1924	*The Iron Horse* John Ford
1925	*Tumbleweeds* (Wm. S. Hart) King Baggott
1925	*Riders of the Purple Sage* (Tom Mix) Lynn Reynolds
1926	*The Red Raiders* (Ken Maynard) Al Rogell
1926	*Lazy Lightnin'* William Wyler
1926	*The Gentle Cyclone* (Buck Jones) W.S. Van Dyke
1926	*The Vanishing American* George B. Seitz
1927	*White Gold* William K. Howard
1929	*The Virginian* Victor Fleming
1930	*Billy the Kid* King Vidor
1930	*The Big Trail* Raoul Walsh

1931	*Cimarron* Wesley Ruggles
1932	*Law and Order* Edward L. Cahn
1933	*To The Last Man* Herbert Bretherton
1936	*The Texas Rangers* King Vidor
1936	*Sutter's Gold* James Cruze
1936	*The Plainsman* Cecil DeMille
1937	*Wells Fargo* Frank Lloyd
1939	*Stagecoach* John Ford
1939	*South of the Border* (Gene Autry) George Sherman
1939	*Union Pacific* Cecil B. DeMille
1939	*Destry Rides Again* George Marshall
1939	*Drums Along The Mohawk* John Ford
1940	*Virginia City* Michael Curtiz
1940	*Jesse James* Henry King
1940	*The Return of Frank James* Fritz Lang
1940	*Kit Carson* George B. Seitz
1940	*The Westerner* William Wyler
1942	*They Died With Their Boots On* Raoul Walsh
1942	*The Great Man's Lady* William Wellman
1942	*The Outlaw* Howard Hughes
1943	*The Ox-Bow Incident* William Wellman
1945	*Duel in the Sun* King Vidor
1946	*My Darling Clementine* John Ford
1947	*The Last Round-Up* (Gene Autry) John English
1947	*Red River* Howard Hawks
1948	*Fort Apache* John Ford
1948	*The Treasure of the Sierra Madre* John Huston
1949	*She Wore a Yellow Ribbon* John Ford
1949	*I Shot Jesse James* Samuel Fuller
1949	*Wagonmaster* John Ford
1950	*The Gunfighter* Henry King
1950	*Rio Grande* John Ford
1950	*Winchester 73* Anthony Mann
1950	*Broken Arrow* Delmer Daves
1952	*The Lusty Men* Nicholas Ray
1952	*The Big Sky* Howard Hawks

1952	*Rancho Notorious* Fritz Lang
1952	*High Noon* Fred Zinneman
1953	*Shane* George Stevens
1953	*The Naked Spur* Anthony Mann
1953	*Hondo* John Farrow
1953	*Silver Lode* Allan Dwan
1954	*Johnny Guitar* Nicholas Ray
1954	*Apache* Robert Aldrich
1955	*The Searchers* John Ford
1955	*The Far Country* Anthony Mann
1955	*Wichita* Jacques Tourneur
1956	*Giant* George Stevens
1956	*Seven Men From Now* Budd Boetticher
1957	*Run of the Arrow* Samuel Fuller
1957	*Forty Guns* Samuel Fuller
1957	*The Tall T* Budd Boetticher
1958	*Buchanan Rides Alone* Budd Boetticher
1958	*The Left-Handed Gun* Arthur Penn
1959	*The Horse Soldiers* John Ford
1959	*One-Eyed Jacks* Marlon Brando
1959	*Rio Bravo* Howard Hawks
1960	*The Magnificent Seven* John Sturges
1960	*The Alamo* John Wayne
1960	*Heller in Pink Tights* George Cukor
1960	*Cimarron* Anthony Mann
1961	*Two Rode Together* John Ford
1961	*The Misfits* John Huston
1962	*Lonely Are The Brave* David Miller
1962	*Ride the High Country* Sam Peckinpah
1962	*The Man Who Shot Liberty Valance* John Ford
1963	*How The West Was Won* Henry Hathaway, John Ford
1963	*McLintock* Andrew V. McLaglen
1963	*Hud* Martin Ritt
1964	*Cheyenne Autumn* John Ford
1966	*For A Fistful of Dollars* Sergio Leone
1967	*El Dorado* Howard Hawks
1967	*The Good, The Bad, and the Ugly* Sergio Leone

1967   *The Way West* Andrew V. McLaglen
1967   *Will Penny* Tom Gries
1968   *The Stranger Returns* Sergio Leone
1969   *True Grit* Henry Hathaway
1969   *The Wild Bunch* Sam Peckinpah
1969   *Once Upon A Time in the West* Sergio Leone
1969   *Butch Cassidy and the Sundance Kid* George Roy Hill

D. A List of Western Films by Subject

The Building of the Railroad

The Iron Horse Ford 1924
Union Pacific Cecil B. deMille 1939
Kansas Pacific Ray Nazarro 1953
Canadian Pacific Edwin L. Marin 1949
Santa Fe Irving Pichel 1951
Denver and Rio Grande Byron Haskin 1952

Outlaws

Rancho Notorious Fritz Lang 1952
I Shot Jesse James Sam Fuller 1949
The Return of Frank James Lang 1940
The Left-Handed Gun Arthur Penn 1958
The Outlaw Howard Hughes 1939
Jesse James Henry King 1939
The True Story of Jesse James Nicholas Ray 1957
The Wild Bunch Sam Peckinpah 1969
The Dalton Gang Ford Beebe 1949
Badman's Territory Tim Whelan 1946
The Bad Men of Tombstone Kurt Neumann 1949
The Younger Brothers Edwin I. Marin 1949
3-10 to Yuma Delmer Daves 1957

Injuns

Broken Arrow Delmer Daves 1950
The Savage George Marshall 1951

Across the Wide Missouri William Wellman 1951
Apache Robert Aldrich 1954
Sitting Bull, Sidney, Salkow 1954
Chief Crazy Horse George Sherman 1955
Pillars of the Sky George Marshall 1956
Geronimo Paul H. Sloane 1940
Geronimo Arnold Laven 1962
Taza, Son of Cochise Douglas Sirk 1954
Cheyenne Autumn John Ford 1964
Run of the Arrow Samuel Fuller 1957
Pawnee George Waganer 1957
Colorado Territory Raoul Walsh 1949
The Devil's Doorway Anthony Mann 1950
The Red Man and the Child
Indian Land Grab
Lo, The Poor Indian
Braveheart 1926

Comedies and Parodies

Destry Rides Again George Marshall 1939
Red Garters George Marshall 1954
Son of Paleface Frank Tashlin 1952
Go West (Marx Bros.) Edward Buzzell 1940
Way Out West (Laurel & Hardy) James W. Horne
    1937
Buck Benny Rides Again Mark Sandrich 1940
The Paleface Norman Z. McLeod 1948
Pardners (Martin & Lewis) Norman Taurog 1956
Ride 'Em Cowboys (Abbott & Costello) Arthur Lubin
Alias Jesse James Norman Z. McLeod 1959
Out West Fatty Arbuckle 1918
My Little Chickadee (W.C. Fields & Mae West) Eddie
    Cline 1940
The Stooges Go West (Gold Raiders) Edwards
    Bernds 1951
Carry On, Cowboy Gerald Thomas 1966
Cat Ballou (Jane Fonda, Nat (King) Cole, Elliot
    Silverstein 1965
True Grit (John Wayne) Henry Hathaway 1969

Support Your Local Sheriff Bud Yorkin 1969

The Cavalry

She Wore a Yellow Ribbon Ford 1949
Fort Apache Ford 1948
Sgt. Rutledge Ford 1960
Rio Grande Ford 1950
A Distant Trumpet Raoul Walsh 1964
Cavalry Scout Lesley Selander 1951
They Died With Their Boots On Walsh 1944
Bugles In The Afternoon Roy Rowland 1954
Thunder of Drums Joseph Newman 1961
The Last Frontier Anthony Mann 1955
Indian Fighter Andre de Toth 1955
Escape From Ft. Bravo John Sturges 1953
Major Dundee Sam Peckinpah 1965

The Modern West

The Misfits John Huston 1961
The Lusty Men Nicholas Ray 1952
A Lady Takes A Chance William A. Seitzer 1943
Return of the Texan Delmer Daves 1952
Bronco Buster Delmer Daves 1952
Hud Martin Ritt 1963
Bucking Broadway John Ford 1917
The Cowboy and the Lady H.C. Potter 1938
Jim Thorpe, All American Michael Curtiz 1951
Rodeo William Beaudine 1952
The Rounders Burt Kennedy 1937
Giant George Stevens 1937
Singing Spurs Ray Nazarro 1948

Musicals

Seven Brides for Seven Brothers Stanley Donen 1954
Annie Get Your Gun George Sidney 1950
The Harvey Girls George Sidney 1946
The Kissing Bandit Laslo Benedek 1948

Calamity Jane David Butler 1953
The Second Greatest Sex George Marshall 1955
Paint Your Wagon
Oklahoma

The Marshal (Sheriff)

Rio Bravo Hawks 1959
My Darling Clementine Ford 1946
El Dorado Hawks 1967
High Noon Fred Zinneman 1952
The Return of Draw Egan
The Tin Star Anthony Mann 1957
Gunfight at the OK Corral John Sturgis 1957
Wichita Jacques Tourneur 1955
Last Train From Gun Hill John Sturges 1959

Cowboys and Cattle Kings

Man Without A Star King Vidor 1954
Cowboy Delmer Daves 1957
These Thousand Hills Richard Fleisher 1962
The Sheepman George Marshall 1958
Jubal Delmer Daves 1956
Red River Hawks 1948
Man From Laramie Mann 1954
Duel in the Sun King Vidor 1947
Tribute to a Bad Man Robert Wise 1956

Gunmen

The Gunfighter Henry King 1950
The Fastest Gun Alive Russell Rouse 1956
The Last of the Fast Guns George Sherman 1958
The Gunman's Walk Phil Karlson 1958
Saddle the Wind Robert Parrish 1958
Shane George Stevens 1953
Buchanan Rides Alone Budd Boetticher 1958
Invitation to a Gunfighter Richard Wilson

Pioneers and Settlers

The Covered Wagon James Cruze 1926
Wagonmaster Ford 1950
Westward Ho! (Disney Production)
Brigham Young, Frontiersman Henry Hathaway 1940
Drums Along the Mohawk Ford 1939
Cimarron Wesley Ruggles 1931
How The West Was Won Ford, Hathaway & Marshall 1963
The Last Wagon Delmer Daves 1956
Two Rode Together Ford 1961
Shane George Stevens 1953
The Big Trail Raoul Walsh 1930
Kit Carson George B. Seitz 1940
California John Farrow 1946

Serials

Liberty Jacques Jaccard & Henry MacRae 1916 (Universal)
The Fighting Trail William Duncan 1917 (Vitagraph)
Lass of the Lumberlands J.P. McGowan & Paul C. Hurst 1916 (Mutual)
The Brass Bullet Ben Wilson 1918 (Universal)
The Masked Rider Aubrey M. Kennedy 1919 (Arrow)
The Terror of the Range Stuart Paton 1919 (Pathe)
The Moon Riders Reeves Eason & Albert Russell 1929 (Universal)
North of the Rockies George Marshall 1920 (Pathe)
Vanishing Trails Leon de la Mothe 1920 (Canyon Picture Corp.)
The Avenging Arrow William J. Bowman & W.S. Van Dyke 1921 (Pathe)
The Purple Riders William Bertram 1921 (Vitagraph)
The White Horseman Ford Beebe 1921 (Universal)
Terror Trail Ed Kull 1921 (Universal)

Winners of the West Edward Laemmule 1921

The Riddle Rider William Craft 1921 (Universal)

In The Days of Buffalo Bill Edward Laemmule 1922
(Universal)

White Eagle (W.S. Van Dyke & Fred Jackman 1922
(Pathe)

Ghost City Jay Marchant 1923 (Universal)

In The Days of Daniel Boone William Craft 1923
(Universal)

The Oregon Trail Edward Laemmule 1923
(Universal)

Ruth of the Range Ernest C. Wade 1923 (Pathe)

The Santa Fe Trail Ashton Dearholt & Robert Dillon

Days of '49 Jacques Jaccard & Ben Wilson 1924
(Arrow)

Galloping Hoofs George B. Seitz 1924 (Pathe)

Leatherstocking George B. Seitz 1924 (Pathe)

North of the Rockies George Marshall 1920 (Pathe)

The Fighting Ranger Henry MacRae & Jay
Marchant 1930 (Universal)

Battle With Kit Carson Armand Schaeffer & Reeves
Eason 1933

The Painted Stallion Ray Taylor, William Witney,
Alan James 1937 (Republic)

Zorro Rides Again John English & Wm. Witney 1937
(Republic)

The Lone Ranger English & Witney 1938 (Republic)

The Adventures of Red Ryder English & Witney 1940
(Republic)

The Great Adventures of Wild Bill Hickock 1938
(Columbia)

The Ghost of Zorro Fred C. Bannon 1949

Overland With Kit Carson Sam Nelson 1939
(Columbia)

Jesse James Rides Again Fred C. Bannon & Thomas
Carr 1947

Riders of the Plains Jacques Jaccard 1924 (Arrow)

10 Scars Make A Man William Parke 1924 (Pathe)

Way of a Man George B. Seitz 1924 (Pathe)

Ace of Spades Herbert McRae 1925 (Universal)
Fighting Ranger Jay Marchant 1925 (Universal)
Idaho Robert F. Hill 1925 (Pathe)
Wild West Robert F. Hill 1925 (Pathe)
The Bar-C Mystery Robert F. Hill 1926 (Universal)
Fighting With Buffalo Bill Ray Taylor 1926 (Universal)
The Return of the Riddle Rider Robert F. Hill (Universal)
Whispering Smith Rides Ray Taylor 1928 (Universal)
The Mystery Rider Jack Nelson 1928 (Universal)
The Scarlet Arrow Ray Taylor 1928 (Universal)
The Vanishing Rider Ray Taylor 1928 (Universal)
The Vanishing West Richard Thorpe 1928 (Mascot)
A Final Reckoning Ray Taylor 1929 (Universal)
The Indians Are Coming Henry McRae 1930 (Universal)

E. *French Critics Select the Ten Best Westerns*

Compilation of the movies mentioned in the Ten Best Westerns lists in *Le Western* rank based on the number of citations in the lists of the 27 critics:

1. *Johnny Guitar* Nicholas Ray
2. *Rio Bravo* Howard Hawks
3. *The Big Sky* Howard Hawks
4. *The Naked Spur* Anthony Mann
    Rancho Notorious Fritz Lang
    Man Without A Star King Vidor
5. *My Darling Clementine* John Ford
    The Left-Handed Gun Arthur Penn
    The Searchers John Ford
    Ride The High Country Sam Peckinpah
6. *Silver Lode* Allan Dwan
    Red River Howard Hawks
    Duel In The Sun King Vidor
    The Hanging Tree Delmer Daves
    Run of The Arrow Sam Fuller

   Seven Men From Now Budd Boetticher
7. *The Last Hunt* Richard Brooks
   The Far Country Anthony Mann
   Colorado Territory Raoul Walsh
   Wagonmaster John Ford
   The Unforgiven John Huston
   Man of the West Anthony Mann
   Heller in Pink Tights George Cukor
8. *Man From Laramie* Anthony Mann
   The Plainsman Cecil B. DeMille
   Western Union Fritz Lang
   Winchester 73 Anthony Mann
   Warlock Edward Dmytryk
   They Died With Their Boots On Raoul Walsh
   The Last Frontier Anthony Mann
   The Last Wagon Delmer Daves
   River of No Return Otto Preminger
9. *Stagecoach* John Ford
   The Outlaw Howard Hughes
   Billy the Kid King Vidor
   Comanche Station Budd Boetticher
   The Wonderful Country Robert Parrish
   Wichita Jacques Tourneur
   3 Hours To Yuma Delmer Daves
   The Magnificent Seven John Sturges
   Gunfight At The OK Corral John Sturges
   Tennessee's Partner Allan Dwan
10. *Backlash* John Sturges
   Lonely Are The Brave David Miller
   Shane George Stevens
   The Tin Star Anthony Mann
   The Horse Soldiers John Ford
   Silver River Raoul Walsh
   A King and Four Queens Raoul Walsh
   The Misfits John Huston
   Union Pacific Cecil B. DeMille
   The Covered Wagon James Cruze
   The Indian Fighter Andre de Toth
   Rio Conchos Gordon Douglas
   Major Dundee Sam Peckinpah

Westward the Women William Wellman
Dallas Stuart Heisler
Jesse James Henry King
Buffalo Bill William Wellman
Bend Of The River Anthony Mann
Broken Arrow Delmer Daves
Run For Cover Sam Fuller
Yellowstone Kelly Gordon Douglas
The Law and Jack Wade John Sturges
The Sheriff of Fractured Jaw Raoul Walsh
Pursued Raoul Walsh
Forty Guns Sam Fuller
The Unconquered Cecil B. DeMille
A Distant Trumpet Raoul Walsh
One-eyed Jacks Marlon Brando
Two Rode Together John Ford
The Sheep Man George Marshall
Last Train from Gun Hill John Sturges
Apache Robert Aldrich
The Iron Horse John Ford
The Singer Not The Song Roy Baker
Yellow Sky William Wellman
The Treasure of the Sierra Madre John Huston
The Gold Rush Charlie Chaplin
Go West Buster Keaton
The True Story of Jesse James Nicholas Ray
Buchannan Rides Alone Budd Boetticher
The Devil's Doorway Anthony Mann
The Gunfighter Henry King
Fort Bravo John Sturges
Taza, Son Of Cochise Douglas Sirk

F. Television Westerns
(Dates given are for first year of appearance)

Hop-along Cassidy 1947
Gene Autry 1947
Roy Rogers 1951
The Lone Ranger 1948
Annie Oakley

The Cisco Kid
Gabby Hayes
Action in the Afternoon
Range Rider
Wild Bill Hickock
Brave Eagle
26 Men
Judge Roy Bean
Tales of the Texas Rangers
Death Valley Days
The Life and Legend of Wyatt Earp
Cheyenne 1955
Gunsmoke 1955
Frontier 1955
Broken Arrow
Dick Powell's Zane Grey Theater
The Adventures of Jim Bowie
Have Gun, Will Travel
Wells Fargo
Sugarfoot
Wagon Train 1957
Colt .45
Lawman
Tombstone Territory
Wanted—Dead or Alive 1958
The Rifleman
The Texan
Bat Masterson
Maverick 1957
Cimarron City
Rawhide
Bonanza 1959
The Deputy 1959
Wichita Town 1959
Laramie 1959
Bronco 1959
Johnny Ringo
The Virginian
Laredo
A Man Called Shenandoah

The Wild Wild West
The Outcasts
Guns of Will Sonnett
The High Chaparral
Rin Tin Tin
Zorro

"Television westerns drive me nuts."

Gene Autry

G. *A Selected List of Western Pulp Magazines*

WESTERN PULP MAGAZINES IN THE EARLY '40s

FROM: Matthieu, Arron M. and Jones, Ruth A. (eds.)
Writer's Market. Cincinnati: Writer's Digest Magazine, 1945,
pp. 132-136.

Hanrahan, John Keith. *The Literary Market Place.* New
York: R.R. Bowker Co., 1940 (vol. 1), pp. 32-34.

The Literary Market Place (vol. 4), 1945, pp. 96-98.

Ace-High Western Stories (Fictioneers)
Action Packed Western (Double Action Group)
Best Westerns (American Fiction Group)
Big Book Western Magazine (Popular Publications
Group)
Blue Ribbon Western (Double Action Group)
Complete Northwest (Double Action Group)
Complete Cowboy
Complete Western Book Magazine (American
Fiction Group)
Cowboy Short Stories (Double Action Group)
Dime Western (Popular Publishing Company)
Doc Savage (S & S All Fiction Group)
Double Action Western (Double Action Group)
Exciting Western (The Thrilling Group)
Famous Western (Double Action Group)

Fifteen Western Tales
44 Western (Popular Publishing Company)
Frontier Stories
Lariat Story Magazine (Newsstand Fiction Unit)
New Western (Fictioneers)
Popular Western (The Thrilling Group)
Range Riders Western (The Thrilling Group)
Real Western (Double Action Group)
Red Seal Western (Ace Fiction Group)
Rio Kid Western (Double Action Group)
Smashing Western (Double Action Group)
Star Western Magazine (Popular Publishing Group)
Ten Story Western (Popular Publishing Group)
Texas Rangers (The Thrilling Group)
Thrilling Western (The Thrilling Group)
Two Gun Western Novels (American Fiction Group)
Variety Western (Ace Fiction Group)
Western Aces (Ace Fiction Group)
Western Action (Double Action Group)
Western Story (S & S All Fiction Group)
Western Trails (Ace Fiction Group)
Western Yarns (Double Action Group)
Wild West Weekly (All Fiction Field)
Northwest Romances
Ranch Romances (Newsstand Fiction Unit)
Rangeland Romances (Popular Publishing Company)
Rodeo Romances (The Thrilling Group)
Romantic Range (S & S All Fiction Group)
Thrilling Ranch Stories (The Thrilling Group)

H. STUDIES OF THE WESTERN NOVEL AND FILM

Adams, Andy, "Western Interpreters." *Southwest Review,* Vol. X (Oct. 1924).

Agnew, Seth M. "Destry Goes on Riding—or—Working the Six-Gun Lode." *Publisher's Weekly,* Vol. 162 (Aug. 23, 1952), pp. 746-751.

Alpert, Hollis. "Westerns With The Willies." *Saturday Review,* Vol. 39 (April 28, 1956), p. 23.

Barker, Warren J., M.D. "The Stereotyped Western Story: Its Latent Meaning and Psychoeconomic Function." *Psychoanalytic Quarterly* Vol. 24 (1955), pp. 270-280.

Barsness, John A. "A Question of Standard." *Film Quarterly*, Vol. XXI, no. 1 (Fall 1967), pp. 32-37.

Bazin, Andre. "Le Western." *Qu'est-ce Que Le Cinema*, Vol. III, Cinema et Sociologie (Paris: Editions de Cerf, 1961).

Blacker, Irwin R. (ed.). *The Old West in Fiction* (New York: Ivan Oblensky Inc., 1961).

Blair, Walter and Meine, Franklin J. (eds.) *Half Horse, Half Alligator. The Growth of the Mike Fink Legend* (Chicago: Univ. of Chicago Press, 1956).

Boatright, Mody C. "The American Myth Rides the Range: Owen Wister's Man on Horseback." *Southwest Review*, Vol. 36, No. 3 (Summer 1951).

Bogdanovitch, Peter. *John Ford* (London: Studio Vista Ltd., 1967).

Bosworth, A.R. "The Golden Age of Pulps." *Atlantic*, Vol. 208 (July 1961), pp. 57-60.

Botkin, B.A. (ed.) *A Treasury of American Folklore. Stories, Ballads, and Traditions of the People* (New York: Crown Publishers, 1944).

Boutell, C.B. "Hi-Yo Silver Lining!" *Nation*, Vol. 152 (Jan 11, 1941), pp. 44-45.

Boynton, H.W. "Word on the Genteel Critic: Owen Wister's Quack Novels and Democracy." *Dial*, Vol. 59 (Oct. 14, 1915), pp. 303-306.

Branch, E. Douglas. *The Cowboy and His Interpreters* (New York: D. Appleton, 1926).

Cracroft, Richard H. "The American West of Karl May. *American Quarterly*, Vol.XIX, No. 2, pt. 1 (Summer 1967), pp. 249-258.

Crisman, G. "Wild and Wooly: How to Tell A Good Western from A Bad One." *Scholastic*, Vol. 34 (May 27, 1939), pp. 21E-22E.

Davis, David Brion. "Ten-Gallon Hero." Hennig Cohen, ed. *The American Experience* (Boston: Houghton Mifflin, 1968).

Dimrock, A.W. "A Real Wild West Show." *Harper's Weekly*, Vol. L (Dec. 8, 1906).

Dobie, J. Frank. "Andy Adams, Cowboy Chronicler." *Southwest Review*, Vol. XI (Jan. 1926), 92-101.

Dobie, J. Frank, ed. *Legends of Texas* (Austin: Texas Folk-Lore Society, 1924).

Durham, Philip and Jones, Everett L. (eds.) *The Frontier in American Literature* (New York: Odyssey, 1969).

Durham, Philip. "A General Classification of 1,531 Dime Novels." *The Huntington Library Quarterly* Vol. VII (1955), 287-291.

Elkin, Frederick. "The Psychological Appeal of the Hollywood Western." *The Journal of Educational Sociology*, Vol. 24 (Oct. 1950), pp. 72-86.

Emery, P.E. "Psychological Effects of the Western Film: A Study in Television Viewing." *Human Relations*, Vol. 12, no. 3 (1959), pp. 195-231.

Eyles, Allen. *The Western* (New York: Barnes, 1967).

Fenin, George N. and Everson, William K. *The Western: From Silents to Cinerama* (New York: Orion, 1962).

Fiedler, Leslie. *Love and Death in the American Novel* (New York: Criterion, 1960). *The Return of the Vanishing American* (New York: Stein & Day, 1968).

Fishwick, Marshall. *"The Cowboy: America's Contribution to the World's Mythology."* *Western Folklore,* Vol. 11, No. 2. (April 1952).

Folsom, James C. *The American Western Novel* (New Haven: College and University Press, 1966).

Folsom, James C. *Timothy Flint* (New York: Twayne Publishers, 1965).

Ford, Charles. *Histoire du Western* (Paris: Editions Pierre Horay, 1964).

Fussell, Edwin. *Frontier: American Literature and The American West* (Princeton: Princeton Univ. Press, 1965).

Gehman, R.B. "Blood and Thunder." *Colliers* Vol. 124 (Oct. 15, 1949), p. 32.

Gehman, R.B. "Deadwood Dick to Superman." *Science Digest* 25 (June 1949), pp. 52-57.

Gruber, Frank. *The Pulp Jungle* (Los Angeles: Sherbourne Press, 1967).

Harvey, Charles M. "The Dime Novel in American Life." *Atlantic Monthly*, Vol. 100 (July 1907), pp. 37-45.

Hazard, Mrs. Lucy Lockwood. *The Frontier in American Literature* (New York: Crowell, 1927).

Hoig, Stan. *The Humor of the American Cowboy*. (New York: New American Library, 1960 zfirst ed., 1958D).

"Hollywood Rides Again." *New York Times Magazine* (August 19, 1945), pp. 16-17.

Homans, Peter. "Puritanism Revisited: An Analysis of the Contemporary Screen-Image Western." *Studies in Public Communication*, No. 3 (Summer 1961), pp. 73-84.

Hopkins, T.J. "Writing the Western. *Writer* 60 (Dec. 1947), pp. 436-438.

Hutchinson, W.H. *The Life & Personal Writings of Eugene Manlove Rhodes. A Bar Cross Man* (Norman: University of Oklahoma Press, 1956).

Julian, H. "Real Fiction in Western Stories." *Saturday Review*, 22 (July 13, 1940), pp. 13-15, discussion Aug. 3, Aug. 17.

Karolides, Nicholas J. *The Pioneer in the American Novel* (Norman: University of Oklahoma Press, 1964).

Keiser, Albert. *The Indian in American Literature* (New York: Oxford, 1933).

Kitses, Jim. *Horizons West*. Anthony Mann, Budd Boetticher, Sam Peckinpah: Studies of Authorship Within the Western. Bloomington: Indiana University Press, 1969, Cinema One Series.

Knight, Arthur. "Westerns Ho!" *Saturday Review* 35 (March 1, 1952), p. 23.

Knight, Arthur. "Three From The West." *Saturday Review*, Vol. 38 (July 30, 1955), p. 26.

Lardner, John. "The Hybrid West." *The New Yorker*, Vol. 33 (Jan. 18 and Jan 25, 1958).

Lee, Robert Edison. *From West to East: Studies in the Literature of the American West* (Urbana: University of Illinois Press, 1966).

Lomax, John A. *Cowboy Songs and Other Frontier Ballads*. (New York: Macmilland, several editions).

McCracken, Harold. *George Catlin and the Old Frontier* (New York: Dial, 1959).

McDermott, John Francis. *George Caleb Bingham: River Portraitist* (Norman: University of Oklahoma Press, 1959).

"Magazine West." *Atlantic* Vol. 101 (Feb. 1908), pp. 279-281.

Martin, P. "Bang! Bang! Bang! Three Redskins Bit the Dust." *Saturday Evening Post* Vol. 219 (August 3, 1946), pp. 26-27.

Masin, H. "They Went Thataway." *Scholastic*, Vol. 66 (April 6, 1955), p. 16T.

Meyer, Roy W. *The Middle Western Farm Novel in the 20th Century* (Lincoln: University of Nebraska Press, 1965).

Miller, Alexander. "The 'Western'—A Theological Note." *Christian Century*, Vol. 74 (Nov. 27, 1957), pp. 1409-1410.

Mitry, Jean. *John Ford* (2 vols. Paris: Editions Universitaries, 1954).

Munden, Kenneth J., M.D. "A Contribution to the Psychological Understanding of the Cowboy and His Myth." *American Imago*, Vol. 15, No. 2 (Summer 1958), pp. 103-148.

Nearhood, R. "Western Popularity Deserved." *Library Journal*, Vol. 73 (March 1, 1948).

Noble, David W."Cooper, Leatherstocking and the Death of the American Adam." In Hennig Cohen, ed. *The American Experience* (Boston: Houghton Mifflin, 1968).

Nussbaum, Martin. "Sociological Symbolism of the Adult Western." *Social Forces*, Vol. 39 (Oct. 1960), pp. 25-28.

Parkman, Francis. "The Works of James Fenimore Cooper." *North American Review*, Vol. 74 (1852), pp. 147-161.

Pearce, Roy Harvey. "The Significance of the Captivity Narrative." *American Literature*, Vol. XIX (March, 1947), pp. 1-20.

Pearce, Roy Harvey. "Penny Fiction (Bibliography)." *Quarterly Review*, Vol. 171 (July, 1980), pp. 150-171.

Priestly, J.B. "Books on the Ranch." *Saturday Review of Literature*, Vol. II (Dec. 15, 1934), p. 368.

Remington, Frederic. *Crooked Trails* (New York: 1908).

Remington, Frederic. *Frederic Remington's Own West*. ed. by Harold McCracken (New York: Dial, 1960).

Renner, Frederic G. *Charles M. Russell: A Descriptive Catalogue* (Austin: Univ. of Texas Press, 1966).

Rickenbacker, William F. "60,000,000 Westerners Can't Be Wrong." *National Review*, Vol. 13 (Oct. 23, 1962), pp. 322-325.

Rieupeyrout, Jean-Louis. *La Grande Aventure du Western* (Paris: Editions du Cerf, 1964).

Roe, V.E. "Western Novel." *Overland*, Vol. 88 (Jan. 1930),

p. 9.

Roosevelt, Theodore. *Ranch Life and the Hunting Trail* (New York: 1888).

Rosenberg, B. "Poor Lonesome Unreviewed Cowboy." *Library Journal*, Vol. 85 (Dec. 15, 1960), pp. 4432-3.

Rush, N. Orwin. "Fifty Years of *The Virginian.*" *The Papers of the Bibliographical Society of America*, Vol. XLVI (1952), pp. 99-117.

Russell, Don. *The Life and Legends of Buffalo Bill* (Norman: University of Oklahoma Press, 1960).

Sarris, Andrew. *The American Cinema* (New York: Dutton, 1968).

Schein, Harry. "The Olympian Cowboy." *The American Scholar*, Vol. 24 (Summer 1955), pp. 309-320.

Sell,Henry Blackman, and Weybright, Victor. *Buffalo Bill and the Wild West* (New York: Oxford, 1955).

Shirley, Glenn. *Pawnee Bill: A Biography of Major Gordon W. Lillie* (Albuquerque: University of New Mexico Press, 1953).

Sisk, J.P. "The Western Hero." *Commonwealth*, Vol. 66 (July 12, 1957), pp. 367-369.

Smith, R.W. "The Southwest in Fiction." *Saturday Review*, Vol. 25 (May 16, 1942), pp. 12-13.

Steckmesser, Kent Ladd. *The Western Hero in History and Legend* (Norman: University of Oklahoma Press).

Thompson, Thomas. "Strong, Silent and Stupid." *The Writer*, Vol. 66 (Sept. 1953), pp. 305-306.

Thorp, Nathan Howard. *Songs of the Cowboys* (Boston: Houghton Mifflin Co.

"Le Western." *Time* Vol. 66 (July 4, 1955), p. 70.

"Westerns." *Time*, Vol. 73 (March 30, 1959), pp. 52-54.

"Top Year for Oaters." *Time*, Vol. 47 (April 29, 1946), p. 94. *Time*. "The Six-Gun Galahad." *Time,* Vol. 73 (March 30, 1959), pp. 52-60.

Thombley, W. "Another Western: Owen Wister's Virginian." *Saturday Evening Post*, Vol. 234 (Dec. 23, 1961), pp. 98-101.

Walbridge, Earle F."*The Virginian* and Owen Wister: A Bibliography." *The Papers of the Bibliographical Society of America*, Vol. XLVI (1952), 117-120.

Waldmeir, J.J. "The Cowboy, Knight and Popular Taste."

Southern Folklore Quarterly, Vol. 22 (Sept. 1958), pp. 113-120.

Walker, Warren S. (ed.). *Leatherstocking and the Critics* (Chicago: Scott, Foresman, 1965).

Walker, S. "Let the Indian Be the Hero." *New York Times Magazine.* (April 24, 1960), p. 50.

Warshow, Robert. *The Immediate Experience* (Garden City, N.Y.: Doubleday, 1962).

Waxman, P. "I Learned About America From Deadwood Dick." *Readers Digest*, Vol. 38 (March 1941), pp. 53-55.

Weaver, J.D. "Destry Rides Again and Again and Again." *Holiday*, Vol. 34 (August, 1963), pp. 77-80.

Wecter, Dixon. *The Hero In America* (Ann Arbor: University of Michigan Press, 1963).

Le Western: Sources, themes, mythologies, auteurs, acteurs, filmographies (Paris: Union General d'Editions, 1966).

White, G. Edward. *The Eastern Establishment and the Western Experience* (New Haven: Yale University Press,1968).

Williams, John. "The 'Western': Definition of the Myth." *Nation* Vol. 193 (Nov. 18, 1961), pp. 401-406.

Wister, Owen. "The Evolution of the Cowpuncher." *The Writings of Owen Wister* (New York: Macmillan, 1928), Vol. VI, pp. xix-li.

Wood, Robin. *Howard Hawks* (Garden City, N.Y.: Doubleday, 1968). Cinema World Series.

Young, C. "Reading for Western" (bibliography). *Writer,* Vol. 66 (May 1953), pp. 158-60.

Zanger, Jules. "The Frontiersman in Popular Fiction." In J.F. McDermott (ed.) *The Frontier Re-Examined* (Urbana: University of Illinois Press, 1968).